You've Got Rhythm

read music better by feeling
the beat

A Complete Method

for reading rhythms

by

Anna Dembska

and

Joan Harkness

flying leap
music
1348 71st Street
Brooklyn, NY 11228
(718) 837-0007
fleap@fleap.com

flying leap music

1348 71st Street
Brooklyn, NY 11228
(718) 837-0007
fleap@fleap.com

First edition, 2002

ISBN 1-930664-04-4 (Complete)

ISBN 1-930664-00-1 (Volume 1)

ISBN 1-930664-01-X (Volume 2)

ISBN 1-930664-02-8 (Volume 3)

Library of Congress Card Number: 00-103056

Printed in Canada

Thank You

To Matthew Brady, Atsuko Ezaki, Conal Fowkes, Cynthia Shaw, the Epiphany choir, and the students in Anna's Sightsinging for Scaredy-Cats classes, for putting Talking Music to the test;

To Geoffrey Armes, Raj Bhimani, Louise Carey, Jim Crapotta, Brian Fitzpatrick, Ellen Glanzer, Sulfiati Harris, Jim Hull, Deborah Karpel, Margaret Martin Kvamme, Kelly Ray Meritt, Benedicto Julián Ramos, Mark Riggleman, Sonya Siebert, Milt Stern, Miriam Strasberg, Sonja Thompson, Allyson Tucker, Ellie Tweedy, Laurie Yorr, and Adrienne Wiley, for pointed criticisms and valuable suggestions;

To Charlotte Abbott, Roz Parr, and Betsy Wollheim for their publishing expertise and advice;

To Bachrun LoMele, Betty LoMele, Steven Mertens, and Jay Rogers for contributions of refrigerator poetry,

To our students for innumerable rhythmic adventures;

As always, to Andrea Hawks and Bachrun LoMele.

About the Authors

Soprano and composer **Anna Dembska** has taught voice, musicianship, and performance technique for over 25 years, including at New York University, and as an Artist-in-Residence with the Metropolitan Opera Guild's In-School Program and National Teacher Training. A graduate of Antioch College with a degree in Music and Dance, she has produced and performed her original music and theater works in venues ranging from the Camden, Maine Opera House to Alice Tully Hall, Lincoln Center. She is artistic director and soprano with the vocal quartet, Singin' Local. As soprano soloist, improviser, and music director, she's collaborated with such innovaters as Leroy Jenkins, Lee Nagrin, Lee Ellikson, and Ralph Lee's Mettawee River Company, among many others. She has received composition grants from Meet the Composer, New Dramatists, and The Puffin Foundation. Her "Kore Chant," recorded by Libana, has been performed by countless numbers of vocal ensembles all over the world.

Joan Harkness, graduate of the Juilliard School and the University of Kansas, is a pianist, teacher, and lecturer. She offers private piano instruction in New York City for all levels and ages of students and at the Brooklyn Friends School. She frequently presents workshops and lectures on meter and rhythm for events such as the New York and New Jersey State Music Teachers Association conventions, chapter meetings of the Music Teachers' Association of California, and the Rocky Mountain Professional Workers conference. As a solo and collaborative pianist, she has performed in New York at Alice Tully Hall, Weill Recital Hall, and the Spanish Institute; and in Mexico at the Festival Cultural Zacatecas and Festival Internacional de Puebla. Her lecture-recitals of Mexican and Spanish music have been heard in schools, colleges, and universities throughout the United States. As an interpreter of contemporary music, she has performed in the premieres of works by Leroy Jenkins and Anna Dembska at The Kitchen and Dixon Place in New York City. Ms. Harkness and Ms. Dembska are currently writing an innovative piano method for adult beginners, slated for publication in 2002.

Contents

Introduction 6

Get Rhythm!

Meter 8

Metric Accents 9

Getting into the Metric Groove 10

Slap/Clap/Tap 10

Talking Music 12

Notes 13

Quarter Notes 13

Half Notes 14

Rests 15

   Splash! 16

Whole Rests 17

   A Debatable Tomato 18

   Why Practice Talking Music? 19

Dotted Half Notes 20

   Plum Pudding 21

Whole Notes 22

   Treasure Map 23

The Pickup 24

   A Flower Song 24

Ties 25

Syncopation 26

   Acorns 27

   Fishing Tips 28

   Jams and Jellies 29

Syncopation Without Ties 30

   A Minimalist Classic 31

   Listening 32

   New York Taxi Ride 33

Repeats 34

   Palimpsest 35

   Friday Night Indecision 36

   Physical Music 37

Eighth Notes 38

   Rural Wisdom 39

   Animal Language 40

Birds 41

Eighth Rests 42

   Take-out 43

   How to Have an Adventure 44

Dotted Quarter Notes 45

   California Mountains 46

   The Description of Virginia 47

   The Jumble That Is Life 48

2/2 Time 49

   Georges Codfish 50

Compound Meter

3/8 Time 52

   Rhyme on Its Head 53

First and Second Endings 54

   Thoreau at Walden Pond 55

6/8 Time 56

   Stage-Fright 57

   Apple Torte 58

Hemiola 59

   Questions. Answers? 60

   Improvisation 61

Sixteenth Notes and Rests 62

   Brains 63

   The Ear 64

   To Remove Fruit Stains 65

   Opera Glasses at the Pawn Shop 66

Syncopation Between the Beats

Eighth Note Syncopation in 4/4 Time 68

   Cheer 69

   Work Song 69

   What Music Can Do 70

   George Gershwin 71

   Storms Are Fine Speakers 72

Four Notes in a Beat 73

   Suspending Disbelief 74

   Mexico City Metro 75

Contents (cont.)

Variations on Four Notes in a Beat 76

   Reminds Me of Some Politicians 77

   A Conversation 78

Sixteenth Note Syncopation 79

   The Ragtime King 80

8th Notes In 2/2 Time 81

   Sun-Treader 82

Eighth Note Syncopation In 2/2 Time 83

   An American Collaboration 84

Tuplets, Double Dots, Suspended Meter, and No Meter

Eighth Note Triplets 86

   Random Salad 89

   Crimped Crust Quaker Bread 90

Double Dots 91

   The Dispute 92

   The Hatter and Alice 93

Quarter Note Triplets 94

   Radish 95

Duples in Compound Meter 96

   Insinuating Rhythm 97

Odd Tuplets 98

   Pickles, Relishes and Sauces 99

   Plants 100

Suspending the Meter, and the Breve 101

   A Style of Reading 101

No Meter 102

   How To Sit 102

Irregular and Shifting Meters

5/8 Time 104

   Doctor's Orders 105

   Chávez 106

5/4 Time 107

   Rewards 108

7/8 Time 109

   Percussion 109

Harry Partch 110

Bartók 111

10/8 Time 112

   Thanksgiving Day 112

   Astronomy With an Opera-Glass 113

Shifting Meters 114

   Aaron Copland 115

   Stravinsky 116

   Practice 117

   Advice From a Caterpillar 118

The Tempo Page 119

Partial Bibliograpy for Composers 120

Glossary with 3-Volume Index 124

Introduction

Rhythm is intrinsic to life. We experience it viscerally, every day, in our heartbeats, as we breath, walk, and talk. Rhythm is just as essential to music. It shapes music with an underlying structure, providing cohesion and vitality. It grounds music in that irresistable momentum that jazz musicians call "groove." Yet when it comes to reading music, many students and amateur musicians have difficulty feeling the groove that comes so naturally when we dance, and play or sing by ear.

Everyone Can Get Rhythm

You've Got Rhythm helps you feel the rhythm while you're reading. It combines spoken-word compositions (we call them "Talking Music") with simple and precise metric patterns of hand-slapping, handclapping, and finger-tapping ("Slap/Clap/Tap"). Slap/Clap/Tap moves your body through the weight and shape of each meter. By kinetically experiencing the meter while you read, the "groove" becomes a natural part of reading and playing music.

Why Slap/Clap/Tap?

Slap/Clap/Tap expresses the "personality" of a meter, literally embodying the weight of the metric accents and lightness of the offbeats. And it clearly delineates the ending point of each beat. With Slap/Clap/Tap you always know where you are in the meter. It helps you feel meter and rhythm more precisely and viscerally than tapping your foot, or even conducting.

Why Use Words?

Words are an important musical and teaching element of the Talking Music pieces. The meter of the lyrics underlines the musical rhythm of each piece. We've used lyrics for phrasing, similar to the way melody creates phrases in a piece of music. We've also used rhythmic patterns to interpret, and sometimes comment on, the meanings of lyrics. For these reasons, we feel Talking Music pieces are compositions, rather than mere exercises. Besides making the pieces more musical and fun to do, the words reinforce the metric and rhythmic interplay.

The Tempo Page

Please see The Tempo Page at the end of the book for explanations of a number of common tempo markings used throughout *You've Got Rhythm*.

Making the Most of You've Got Rhythm

If you work through this book step-by-step, you'll gain a comprehensive knowledge and understanding of rhythm. But that's only the beginning. All our students have come up with ways to play with and expand on the material, from performing Talking Music pieces in canon to inventing their own Talking Musics for the rhythms of music they're studying. It's especially fun to practice *You've Got Rhythm* with a group of friends or fellow students. We hope you'll use this method as a jumping-off point to deepen your rhythmic understanding and enjoyment in all your musical adventures.

Get Rhythm!

Slap/Clap/Tap, Talking Music, Meter, Notes, and Rests

2/4, 3/4, 4/4, and 2/2 are simple meters.

Meter is the rhythmic ordering of music into groups of two beats and three beats. The personality of each meter is expressed through metric accents and offbeats.

Slap/Clap/Tap is a system of hand-slapping, -clapping, and -tapping to physically experience the shape and personality of a meter.

Talking Music compositions use words spoken rhythmically in conjunction with Slap/Clap/Tap in order to read music better by feeling the beat!

Notes are the symbols that represent the sounds you play.
For silence, rests are used.

Meter

The rhythms in the world give us our sense of time—night and day, seasons, lunar phases pulling the tides...

Our bodies have rhythms, too: breathing, wake and sleep, and heartbeats, to name a few. The regular beating of your heart is the kind of steady pulse you need to play music.

1. Find the pulse of your heartbeat by sitting quietly and listening. If you can't sense it, feel for the pulse in your wrist or neck.

2. Mark the pulse in your mind, or move a finger or toe along with the beat.

3. Now count on each pulse, counting in groups of two and groups of three:

in two: **1 2   1 2   1 2   1 2   1 2**

in three: **1 2 3   1 2 3   1 2 3   1 2 3**

Meter is the rhythmic ordering of music into groups of two beats and three beats. Meters are organized into **measures** (also called **bars**) by **time signatures** and **bar lines**.

The top number of the time signature tells you how many beats there are in each measure. The bottom number will be explained on page 13.

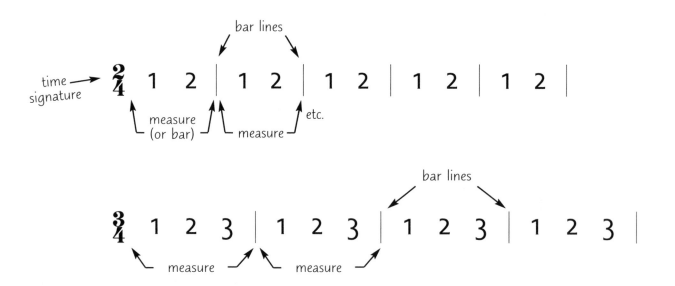

Metric Accents

Each meter has a different feeling from every other. For example, in dance music, a polka has a two-beat feel. It has a very different feeling from a waltz, which is in a meter of three.

The groups of two beats and three beats within a measure make patterns of stronger and weaker accents which give each meter its own distinct personality. We'll refer to these accents as **metric accents**. Understanding and being aware of the beat groupings and metric accents will serve you well for getting rhythm into your body as you read and play music.

Count the following meters out loud, emphasizing the metric accents.

1. No matter what meter you're in, the first beat in a measure has the strongest metric accent. It's called the **downbeat.** In a meter of two:

$$\frac{2}{4} \quad \underline{\underline{1}} \quad 2 \mid \underline{\underline{1}} \quad 2 \mid \underline{\underline{1}} \quad 2 \mid \underline{\underline{1}} \quad 2 \mid \underline{\underline{1}} \quad 2 \mid$$

2. Two groups of two are put together to make a meter of four. The first beat of any group has a metric accent, although not as strong as the downbeat. In 4/4 time, the first beat of the second group of two—the third beat—is an accent, but less strong than the downbeat:

$$\frac{4}{4} \quad \underline{\underline{1}} \quad 2 \mid \underline{3} \quad 4 \mid \underline{\underline{1}} \quad 2 \quad \underline{3} \quad 4 \mid \underline{\underline{1}} \quad 2 \quad \underline{3} \quad 4 \mid \underline{\underline{1}} \quad 2 \quad \underline{3} \quad 4 \mid$$

3. 3/4 is the only meter with a metric accent on a beat other than the first beat of a group. In 3/4, there is one group of three beats, with the strong accent on the downbeat. But the second beat also has an accent—a weaker one.

$$\frac{3}{4} \quad \underline{\underline{1}} \quad \underline{2} \quad 3 \mid \underline{\underline{1}} \quad \underline{2} \quad 3 \mid \underline{\underline{1}} \quad \underline{2} \quad 3 \mid \underline{\underline{1}} \quad \underline{2} \quad 3 \mid$$

Getting into the Metric Groove with
Slap/Clap/Tap

A musician has to use intellect, feelings, and body together to play or sing skillfully and freely. When your body learns a meter and its metric accents, you feel a groove that carries the rhythm, so your mind and emotions are free to read and interpret the music. **Slap/Clap/Tap** helps your body incorporate the metric feel.

While sitting,

> **SLAP** your legs on the strongest beat (always beat 1—the **downbeat**)

> **CLAP** on the next strongest beat (the first beat of a grouping of two or three beats, or beat 2 in 3/4 time)

> **TAP** your thumbs against your index fingers on the weak beat—the **offbeat**.

If you need to hold your music in your lap, Slap on the sides of your legs or on your seat.

Slap   **Clap**   **Tap**

With each of the following meters, count out loud, stressing the metric accents with your voice, as you Slap/Clap/Tap. Feel the weight that Slap and Clap give to the metric accents, and the lightness of the Taps. You'll feel the distinct personality of a meter as you become familiar with it.

Practice each example over and over, *for longer than you think is necessary*, until your body is not only comfortable with the metric groove, but you feel like you will never forget it! The practice on this page is a foundation for all the pieces in this book, and, it might be argued, all the pieces you will ever play or sing!

Some people find it easier if they can visualize the shapes their hands are outlining as they move through the Slap/Clap/Tap patterns. There's a diagram of each shape next to its meter.

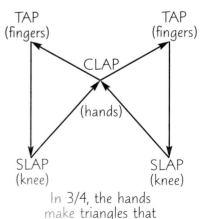

Talking Music

This book is full of pieces of music that use words in rhythmic patterns. We call these "Talking Music." We wrote them to inspire and amuse you with their literary content, while giving you practice in a full spectrum of rhythms.

How to Perform Talking Music and Practice All the Pieces in This Book

1. Read through the words to get familiar with them before you start.

2. Look at the time signature to find the meter and the Slap/Clap/Tap pattern you'll use to perform the piece.

3. Begin to Slap/Clap/Tap in a slow, steady pulse, silently counting the beats of the meter. Feel the weight that Slap and Clap give to the metric accents, and the lightness of the Taps. Slap/Clap/Tap and count—silently or out loud—for one or more bars before starting the piece—musicians call this **"one for nothing"** or "two for nothing." It gets you in the groove before you play the music.

4. Speak each syllable for the length of the note under it. The metric personality will emerge as you Slap/Clap/Tap the beats and speak the words.

5. Focus your eyes on the notes, and look at the words with your peripheral vision.

6. If you make a mistake, keep your hands moving—because the music never stops!—and try to find your way back in again. Let the rhythm of the meter carry you through the piece.

Take Your Time to Keep Your Time

When you're sight-reading a piece for the first time, make your tempo as slow as you need to keep a completely steady, regular beat, regardless of the composer's tempo markings. As you do the piece again and become more familiar with it, speed up the tempo (if necessary). Go a little faster each reading, until you are up to tempo. But don't speed up *during* the piece unless, of course, you see an ***accelerando***!

Notes

Notes are the symbols that represent the sounds you play. They show how long to play a tone, as well as its **pitch**—how high or low it is. In this book, you'll learn about note durations and how they relate to meter.

Quarter Notes

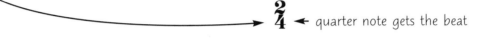

This is the **notehead**.

This is the **stem**.

The lower number of the time signature tells you which note gets one beat. When the number is 4, a quarter note gets one beat. In 2/4 time, there are two quarter notes in each measure. In this book, we refer to any time signature with a 4 on the bottom as "**4 time**."

$\frac{2}{4}$ ← quarter note gets the beat

double bar line means Stop! The End!

Slap/Clap/Tap through these miniature Talking Musics:

TGIF

Weekend Plans

Movement

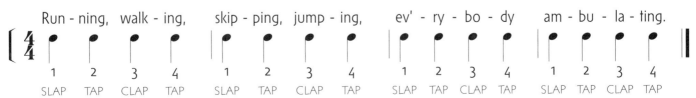

Half Notes

Half notes are held twice as long as quarter notes. In 4 time (3/4, 4/4, and 2/4), half notes have a duration of two beats. The sound continues through the second beat.

Hold the word on a half note all the way through both beats. It's kind of like chanting.

Spring Season

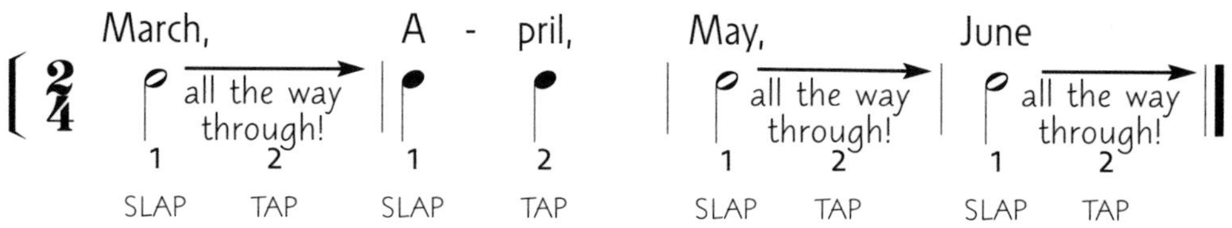

The Big Muddy

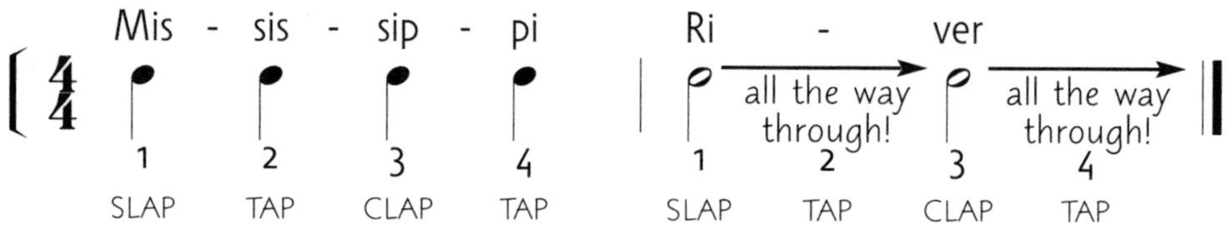

Valentine

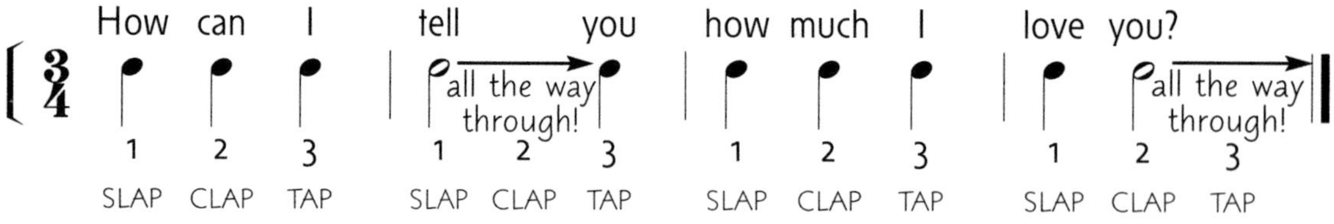

Rests

So far, you've been making and hearing sounds for every note. But for silence, **rests** are used. Each note value has a corresponding rest.

Quarter Rest

A **quarter rest** lasts for the same length as a quarter note: one beat in 4 time.

Perform the Talking Music pieces below. You won't speak during the beats with rests, but continue to Slap/Clap/Tap and count silently on every beat.

Office Supplies

Half Rest

A **half rest** sits on top of a line. It's the same length as a half note.

Night Sky

Fair Weather

Wrong Number

Get into the groove by Slap/Clap/Tapping one or two bars for nothing before you begin to speak. Make your Slap/Clap/Tap tempo as slow as you need to keep a steady beat throughout the piece.

Splash!

adapted from *Pioneer Proverbs: Wit and Wisdom from Early America*

collected by Mary Turner   Joan Harkness

Whole Rests ▬

Whole rests hang down from a line on the staff and indicate a whole measure of rest, regardless of the time signature.

End of the Line

Halloween

A Chorus of Well-Wishers

A Debatable Tomato

from *Burpee's Farm Annual* (1888)

Anna Dembska

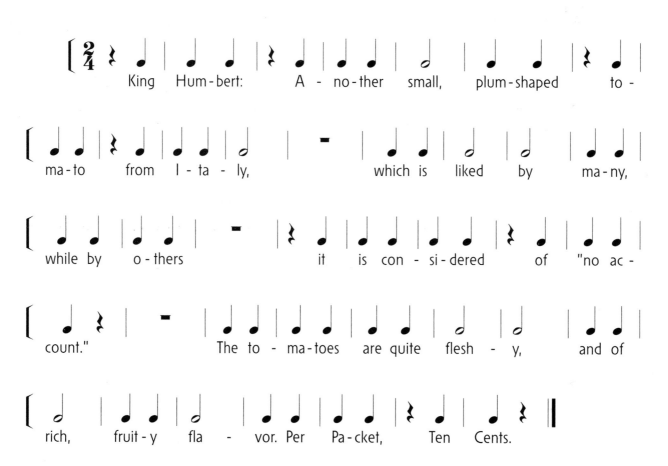

King Hum-bert: A - no-ther small, plum-shaped to-ma-to from I-ta-ly, which is liked by ma-ny, while by o-thers it is con-si-dered of "no ac-count." The to-ma-toes are quite flesh-y, and of rich, fruit-y fla-vor. Per Pa-cket, Ten Cents.

Why Practice Talking Music?

Anna Dembska

Dotted Half Notes 𝅗𝅥. 𝅘𝅥.

Sometimes you'll see a dot next to a note, like the **dotted half notes** above. The dot makes the note longer by half. For example:

A half note lasts for two beats in 2/4, 3/4 and 4/4:   𝅗𝅥 = 2

Half of two beats is one beat, represented by a dot: + · = 1

Add that to the duration of a half note to get three beats: 𝅗𝅥. = 3

Slap/Clap/Tap your way through these miniature Talking Musics. Hold the tone of the word on a dotted half note all the way through to the end of the third beat.

Pianos

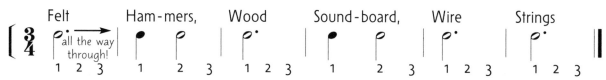

'Nuff said...

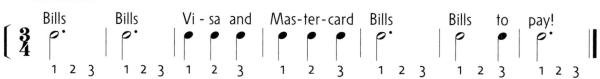

A. M. Choices

Plum Pudding

adapted from *Pioneer Proverbs: Wit and Wisdom from Early America*

Mary Turner

Joan Harkness

Moderato

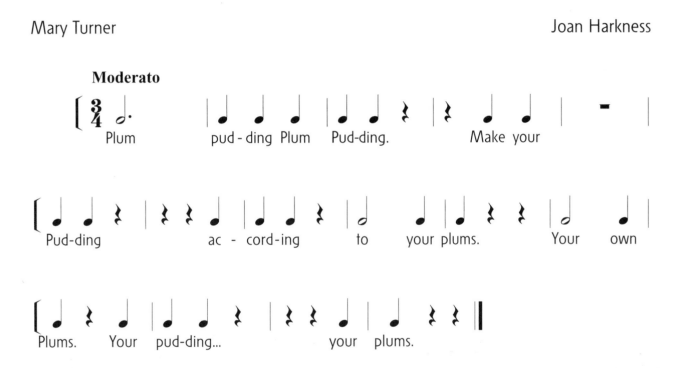

Whole Notes o

In 4/4 time, **whole notes** are held through four beats.

Hold the tone of a whole note all the way through to the end of the fourth beat.

Soccer

Sunset

Treasure Map

Anna Dembska

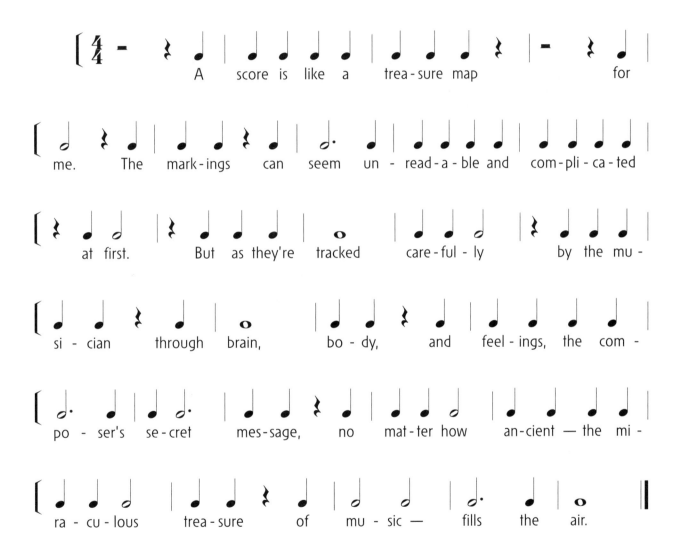

A score is like a trea-sure map for me. The mark-ings can seem un - read-a-ble and com-pli-ca-ted at first. But as they're tracked care-ful - ly by the mu - si - cian through brain, bo - dy, and feel-ings, the com - po - ser's se-cret mes-sage, no mat-ter how an-cient — the mi - ra - cu - lous trea-sure of mu - sic — fills the air.

The Pickup

Not every piece of music starts on beat one.

Here in "A Flower Song," there's only one beat in the first measure, and it's beat four! When the first measure of a piece is **incomplete**—having fewer beats than the time signature indicates—the missing beats are the ones at the beginning of the measure (in this case, beats 1, 2, and 3). So "A Flower Song" begins on beat four (a Tap).

This note begins a musical **phrase** which continues through the third beat of the next measure: "He loves me." A partial measure which begins a phrase is called a **pickup**, an **upbeat**, or an **anacrusis.** In this case, it's one note, but it could include more than one note. And what is a musical phrase? It's like a sentence or a part of a sentence—it's a group of notes that feels complete in itself.

With a pickup, do a few bars for nothing, beginning with a Slap, as usual, and count and Slap/Clap/Tap through the missing beats of the incomplete measure until you get to the Tap of the first note, where you'll begin the piece.

The dotted lines after the **accel.** marking tell you to keep accelerating as long as the dotted line lasts.

A Flower Song

Joan Harkness

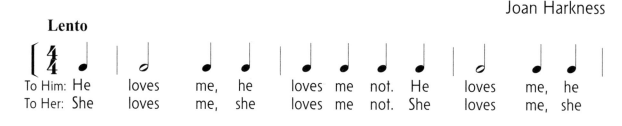

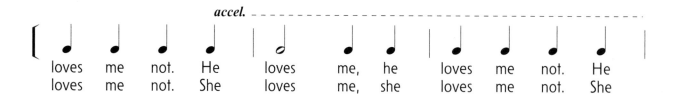

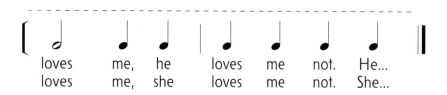

Ties

Notes of the same pitch can be connected with **ties** to make a note of longer length. A tie often connects a note over a barline to a note in the next measure.

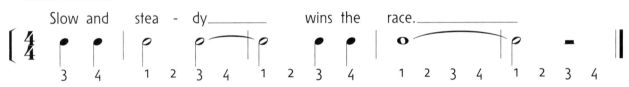

Therefore, hold the vowel of the syllable through all the beats of all the tied notes.

Turtle's Advice

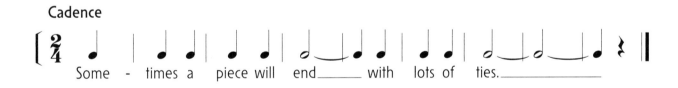

Cadence

Tag

Syncopation

In a **syncopated rhythm**, the music goes against the metric accents, emphasizing the **offbeats**—the Taps instead of the Slaps and Claps.

As you know, a 4/4 measure is made of two groups of two beats, with metric accents on the first beat of each group—beats 1 and 3, the Slap and Clap. When a tie links beats 2 and 3 across the Great Divide between the two groups, it creates **syncopation**. Repeat the following example, stressing the syncopated syllables ("-my", "have" and "yet" in the next example) as you speak, until you clearly hear and feel the syncopation against the metric accents.

Road Trip

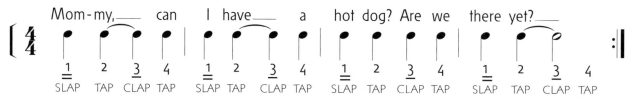

Syncopation can also occur when the last beat of a measure (a Tap, the weakest beat) is tied to the first beat of the next measure (a Slap, the strongest beat). Try this example, stressing the syncopated syllables ("gold," "red," "salt,") and repeating it until you feel the swing of the syncopation.

The Salt Marsh at Neap Tide

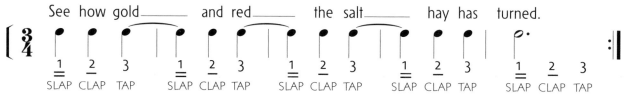

Another way to create syncopation is to put a rest on the metric accent and a note on the unaccented beat (sometimes referred to as a **offbeat**). Try this:

Freeloader

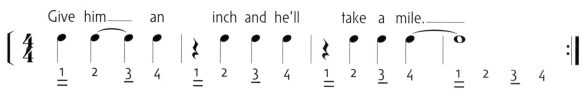

Acorns

Adapted from *Pioneer Proverbs: Wit and Wisdom From Early America*

Collected by Mary Turner

Joan Harkness

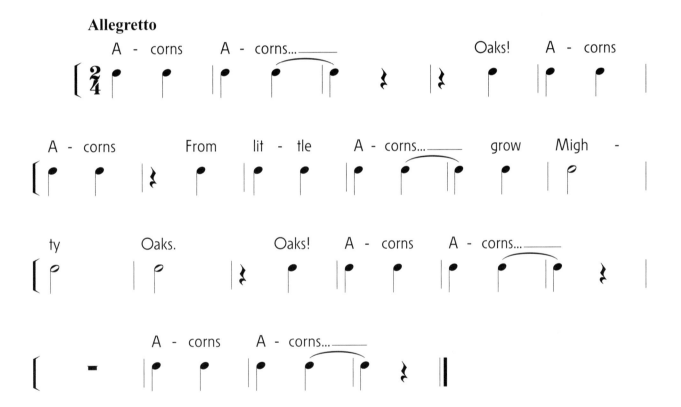

Notice the **fermatas** 𝄐 at the end of "Fishing Tips," and hold the notes longer than their values (see The Tempo Page). For notes with fermatas, Slap/Clap/Tap at the usual tempo, but hold on the last beat.

Fishing Tips

from *The Lake of the Sky—Lake Tahoe* (1915)

George Wharton James   Joan Harkness

Jams and Jellies

from the *1998 Madison County* (Nebraska) *Fairbook*, "Open Class"

Joan Harkness

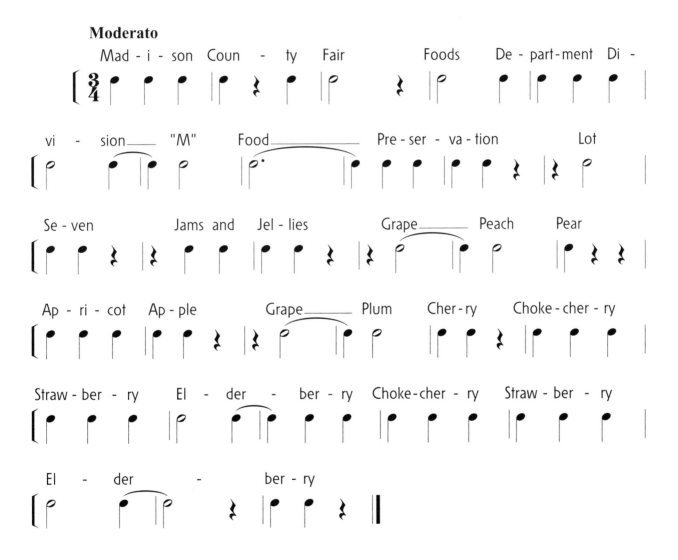

Syncopation Without Ties

Half notes often replace the tied quarters across the Great Divide—but it's still syncopation.
Musicians learn to visually recognize this syncopated pattern as they sight-read.

Road Trip

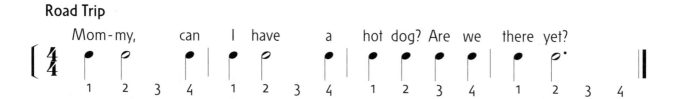

Freeloader

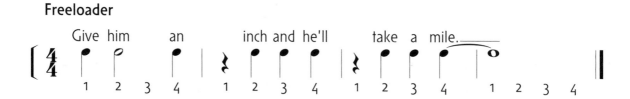

A Minimalist Classic

Anna Dembska

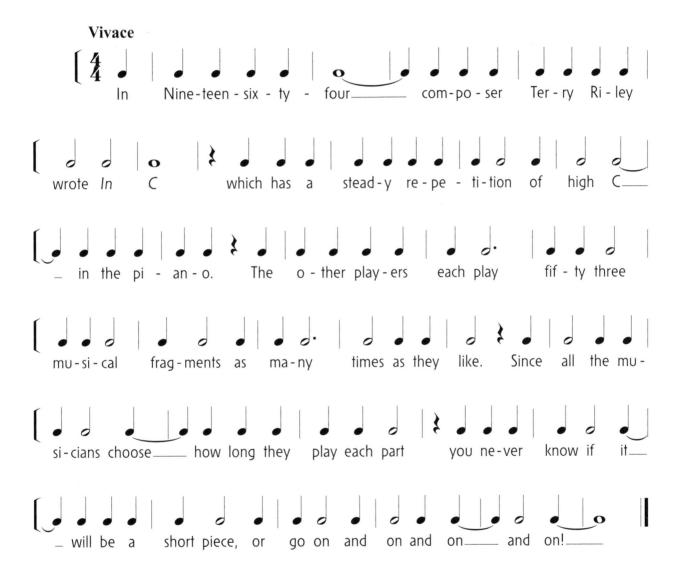

Vivace

In Nine-teen - six - ty - four_____ com-po - ser Ter - ry Ri - ley

wrote *In C* which has a stead-y re-pe - ti-tion of high C_____

_ in the pi - an-o. The o - ther play-ers each play fif - ty three

mu - si - cal frag-ments as ma-ny times as they like. Since all the mu-

si - cians choose_____ how long they play each part you ne-ver know if it_____

_ will be a short piece, or go on and on and on_____ and on!_____

Listening

Anna Dembska

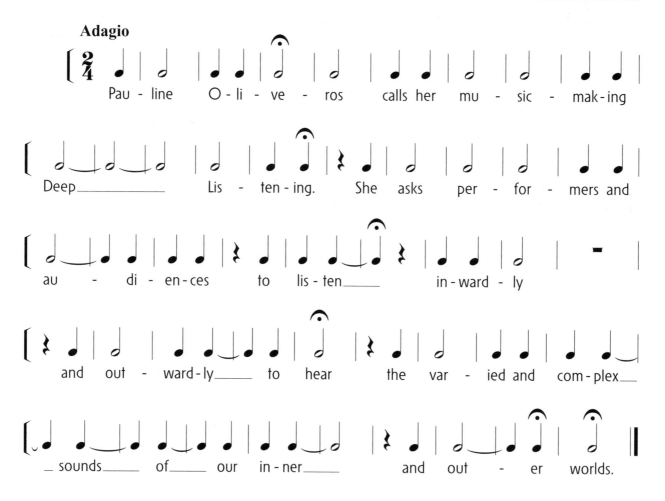

A piece of music may have several different meters within it, so look out for time signature changes. When you come to a new meter, change to its Slap/Clap/Tap pattern. Look ahead so you won't be caught by surprise! As you learn the piece, you'll hear and feel the shifting meters and the changes will feel more natural. By the way, in New York, Houston is pronounced "Howstun."

New York Taxi Ride

Joan Harkness

Presto frenetico

JFK JFK JFK Air - port
Ta - xi! Ta - xi! JFK Belt Park-way Belt Park Con - ey
Is - land Belt Park-way Go - wan - us Go - wan - us B Q E
Stat - ue of Li - ber - ty! Brook - lyn Bridge Brook - lyn East
Side, F D R Drive F D R Drive Hous - ton
Hous - ton West Side, High-way High-way The
Kit - chen Kit - chen Lin - coln Cen - ter Met - ro - pol - i - tan
Op' - ra Puc - ci - ni Tos - ca Tos - ca Vis - si d'art - e!

Repeats

These are **repeat signs**:

first or left repeat sign   second or right repeat sign

Repeat signs tell you to play part of the music again. As you read through the music and encounter the first repeat, don't do anything yet; just remember where it is. (The names we've given them, "left," "first," "right," and "second" are not official names. They're just a way for us to identify them for discussion purposes.)

When you get to the second repeat, go back to the first sign and play the music between it and the second repeat sign again. Then proceed as usual to play the next section of music.

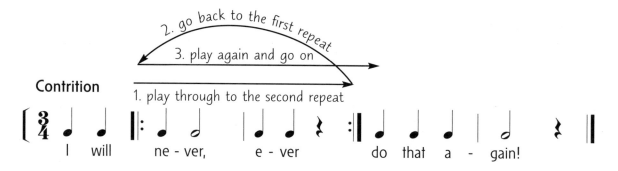

Sometimes you'll see a "second" (right) repeat sign without the first (left) one. In that case, go back to the beginning of the piece and repeat all the music before the repeat sign, then continue on to the next section as usual.

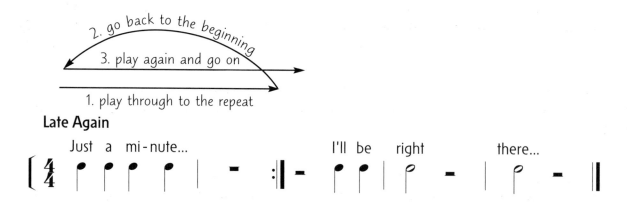

A palimpsest is something that had been written on, then erased, then written on again, as described in this Talking Music.

Palimpsest

from *A Thousand-Mile Walk to the Gulf* (1912)

John Muir

Joan Harkness

Moderato

When a page is writ-ten o-ver but once it may

be ea-si-ly read; but if it be writ-ten o-ver and

o-ver with cha-rac-ters of ev'-ry size and style, it

soon be-comes un - read-ab-le.... Our li - mi-ted

pow-ers are si-mi-lar-ly per-plexed and o - ver - taxed in

read-ing the in - ex - haus-ti-ble pa - ges of na-ture, for

they are writ-ten o-ver and o-ver un - coun-ta-ble times. All to-

ge-ther form the one grand pa - limp-sest of the world.

This piece has a **verse—refrain** (sometimes known as the **chorus**) form. Begin with the refrain, then alternate with the verses (verse 1—refrain—verse 2—refrain, etc.) until finally ending the piece with the refrain.

Friday Night Indecision

Joan Harkness

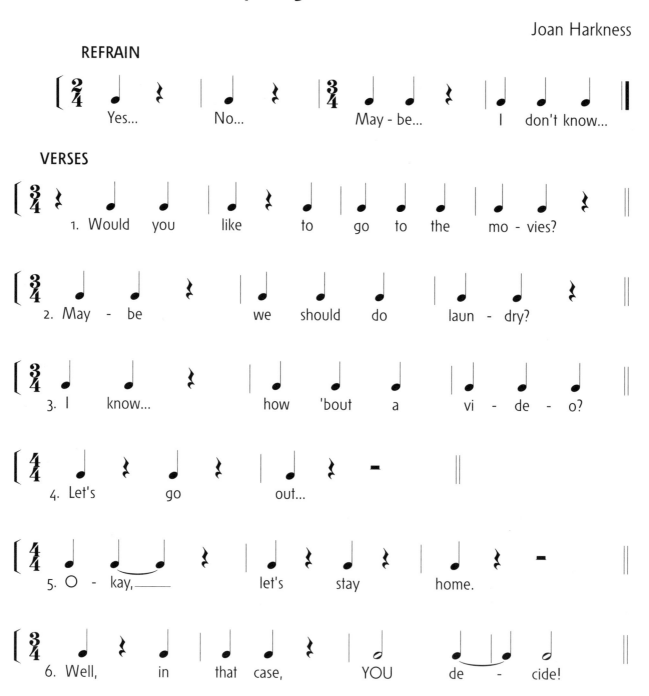

In this piece for two voices, some consonants get their own notes for percussive effect.

Physical Music

Anna Dembska

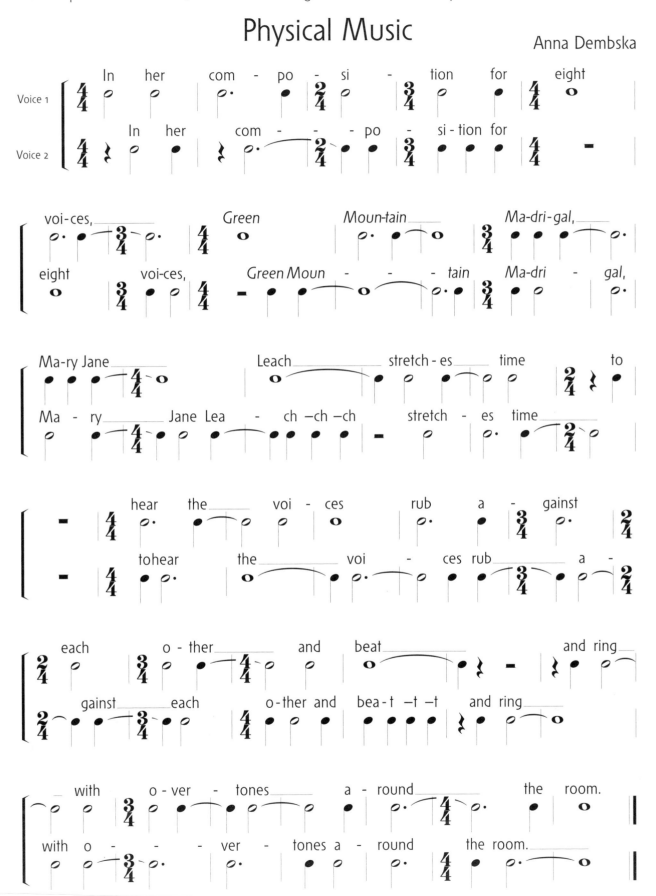

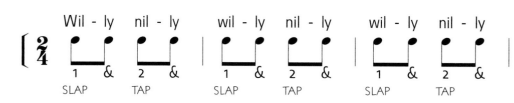

Eighth Notes

A beat can be divided into two equal halves. When you divide a quarter note in half you get two **eighth notes**: ♪♪ So in 2/4, 3/4, and 4/4 time, you can have two eighth notes in the duration of one beat.

1. Slap/Tap. Say "wil" on the Slap and "nil" on the Tap:

2. Now add "y" in between each count. Slap/Tap is the same as in Step 1, but there are two notes in each beat, so you'll speak two syllables for each Slap or Tap. Because an eighth is half of a beat, musicians use "and" (abbreviated "&") to count it. Try the example a second time, counting " 1 & 2 &" out loud instead of saying "willy nilly."

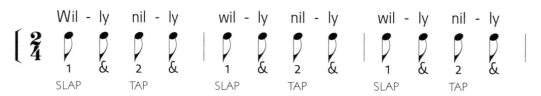

3. Often two eighth notes are **beamed** together so they are grouped into a beat. They sound exactly the same as **flagged** eighths, but help you see the beats. Say "willy nilly" while keeping "1 & 2 &" in your mind.

this is the **beam**

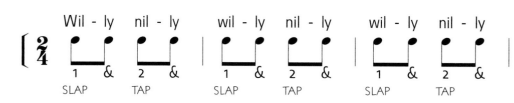

Ice Cream

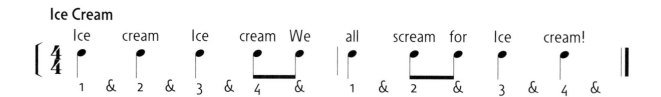

Rural Wisdom

from *Huckleberry Finn* (1884)

Mark Twain (Samuel L. Clemens)   Anna Dembska

Animal Language

from *The Story of Doctor Doolittle* (1920)

Hugh Lofting

Anna Dembska

Birds

adapted from U.S. Fish and Wildlife Service website, Region 6 Listed Species Under Fish and Wildlife Service Jurisdiction By State as of 06/30/98

Joan Harkness

Eighth Rests ⁊

Eighth rests have the same duration as eighth notes.

An eighth note followed by an eighth rest sounds like a shortened quarter note.

Magnetic Poetry 1

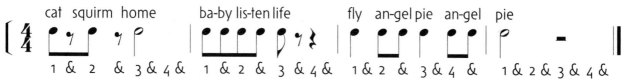

Magnetic Poetry 2

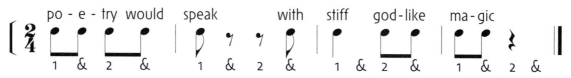

Magnetic Poetry 3

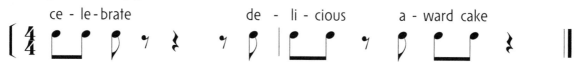

The Channel Islands

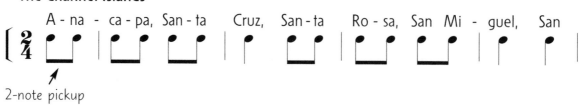

2-note pickup

The symbol **C** (common time) is short-hand for the time signature 4/4, supposedly because 4 beats in a measure is the most "common" meter to be found.

Take-out

Joan Harkness

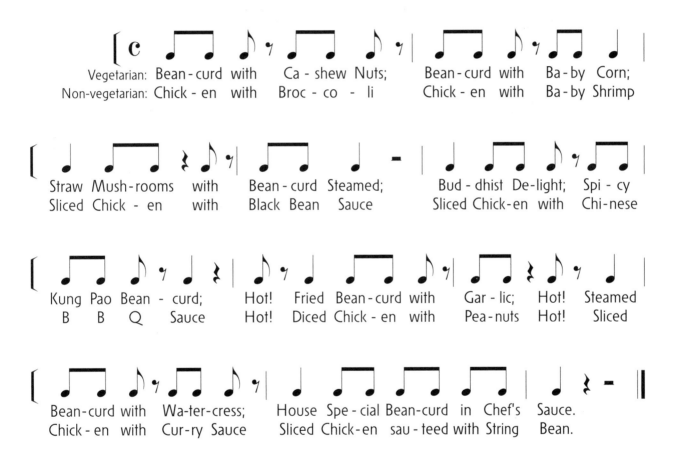

How to Have an Adventure

from *The Lake of the Sky—Lake Tahoe* (1915)

George Wharton James

Joan Harkness

Dotted Quarter Notes

As with a dotted half note, a **dotted quarter note** is longer by half than a regular quarter note.

A quarter note lasts for one beat in 2/4, 3/4 and 4/4:

Half of one beat is one-half beat, represented by a dot:

Add that to the duration of a quarter note to get one-and-a-half beats:

1. Slap/Tap, while saying "wil nil-ly."

2. Now leave out "nil" as you tie the quarter note to the eighth note.

3. Dotted quarter notes standing in for the tied notes sound exactly the same as quarters tied to eighths.

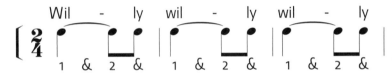

4. Try the opposite; eighth note first:

5. And a dotted quarter after the eighth note:

California Mountains

Joan Harkness

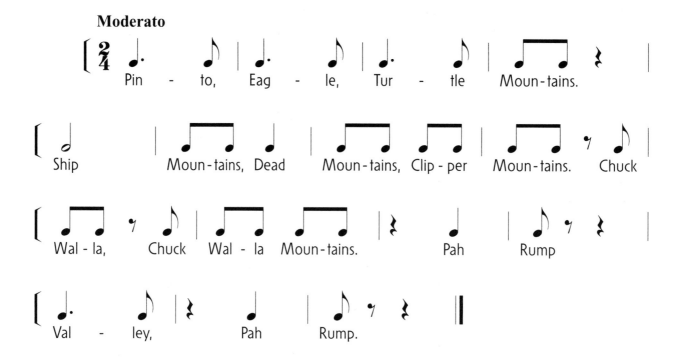

The Description of Virginia

(1612)

Captaine Smith   Anna Dembska

The som-mer is hot as in Spaine; the win-ter colde___ as in Fraunce or Eng - land. The heat of som-mer is in June, Ju - lie, and Au-gust, but com-mon-ly the coole brees - es as - swage the ve-he-men-cie of the heat. The chiefe of win-ter is halfe De-cem - ber, Jan-u-a-ry,___ Fe-bru-a-ry, and halfe March. The colde is ex-treame sharpe, but here the pro-verbe is true that no ex - treame long con - ti-nu-eth. No ex - treame long con - ti-nu-eth.

The Jumble That Is Life

Joan Harkness

Allegro, with spirit

Some - times, you may have no - ticed, life is not neat,

or ti - dy. To - day has parts of yes - ter - day, last

year and next month all mixed up in it. The feel-ings, the sounds and songs, the

spi - rit of those past and fu - ture times are the pre - sent. Charles Ives

lis - tened_____ to the jum - ble_____ that is life and

wrote the mu - sic down. Too com - plex! peo - ple say.

It makes me mad! the mu - si - cians com - plain. But so it is: un -

flin - ching so - nic por - traits of hu - ma - ni - ty.

2/2 Time

When the lower number of the time signature is 2, a half note gets the beat. We call it "**2 time.**"

$\mathbf{2 \atop 2}$ ← 2 beats in a measure

← half (1/2) note gets one beat

There are two metric accents in 2/2 time. 2/2 time is like 4/4 time reduced to its metric accents. That's why you Slap and Clap instead of the Slap and Tap of 2/4 time. Because it's cut down in this way, it's sometimes called **cut time**. The symbol for cut time is common time ($\mathbf{C}$) cut in half:

$$\math¢$$

The relationships between the notes remain the same: whole notes are twice as long as half notes; half notes are twice as long as quarters. So a whole note gets two beats, a quarter note gets half a beat, and an eighth note gets a quarter of a beat!

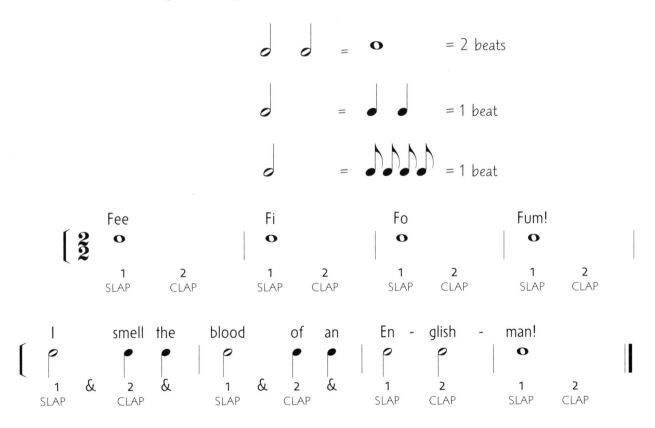

REMEMBER:

Always look at the time signature in every piece so you know how to count and Slap/Clap/Tap.

Georges Codfish

Advertisement from *The Boston Cooking-School Cookbook*, 1st edition (1896)

Anna Dembska

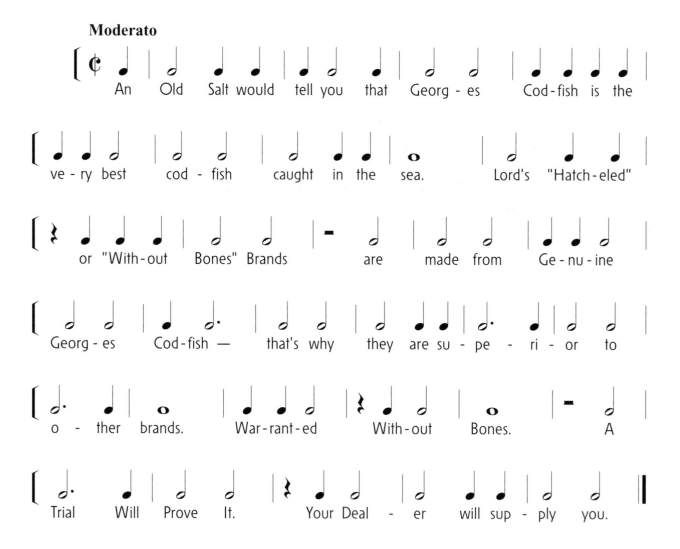

Compound Meter

3/8, 6/8, 9/8 and 12/8

3/8 is a simple meter, like 2/4, 3/4, 4/4, and 2/2.

6/8, 9/8, and 12/8 are compound meters. Compound meters have two or more pulses in a measure, with each pulse containing a group of three beats.

In compound meters in "8 time," there is a metric accent on the first beat of each group of three eighth-note beats.

3/8 Time

When the lower number of the time signature is 8, an eighth note gets the beat.
We call it "**8 time**."

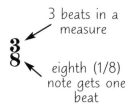

3 beats in a measure

eighth (1/8) note gets one beat

A quarter note now gets two beats. A dotted quarter note gets three. The relationship remains the same:

1. Use Slap/Tap/Tap instead of the Slap/Clap/Tap of 3/4:

Behind Schedule

Run for the bus! We're gon-na be late!

1 2 3 1 2 3 1 2 3 1 2 3
SLAP TAP TAP SLAP TAP TAP SLAP TAP TAP SLAP TAP TAP

The tempo of 3/8 is usually fast. Often it feels so fast that you can count it as one pulse with three subdivisions.

2. Speak the lyrics as you Slap on beat one, skipping the Taps.
   Repeat, getting faster each time, until it feels natural.

   The count in your head will be "1 1 1 1"

Behind Schedule

Run for the bus! We're gon-na be late!

1 1 1 1
SLAP SLAP SLAP SLAP

Because this piece is notated in 3/8 time, its ultimate tempo should have a pulse of one. Practice it first counting three pulses to a bar. Then, as you get more comfortable, try it in "one." The **A tempo** after the *accel.* tells you to go back to the original tempo: the one at which you started.

Rhyme on Its Head

Joan Harkness

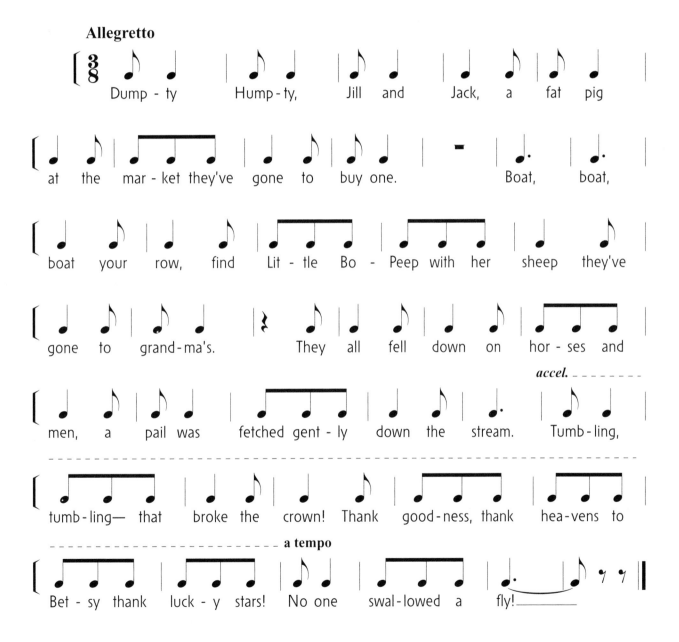

First and Second Endings

Sometimes a phrase is repeated a few times with different endings each time. In these cases, you'll find repeats with **first** and **second** and possibly **third, fourth, fifth,** etc. **endings** appearing above the staves.

a first ending: 1   a second ending: 2

1. First time through, play to the end of the 1st ending (up to the second repeat sign).

2. At the second repeat sign, go back to the first repeat sign and repeat, *up to, but not including,* the first ending.

3. *Jump over* the first ending to the *second* ending, and proceed from there to the end.

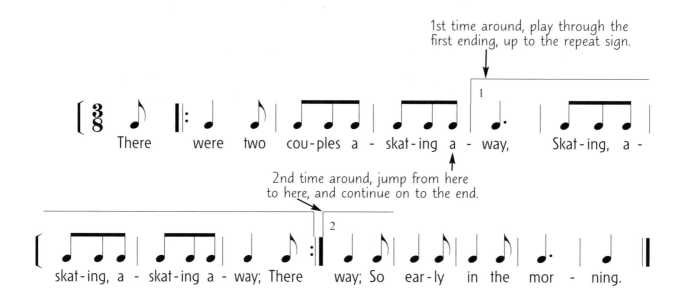

Thoreau at Walden Pond

Henry Thoreau

Anna Dembska

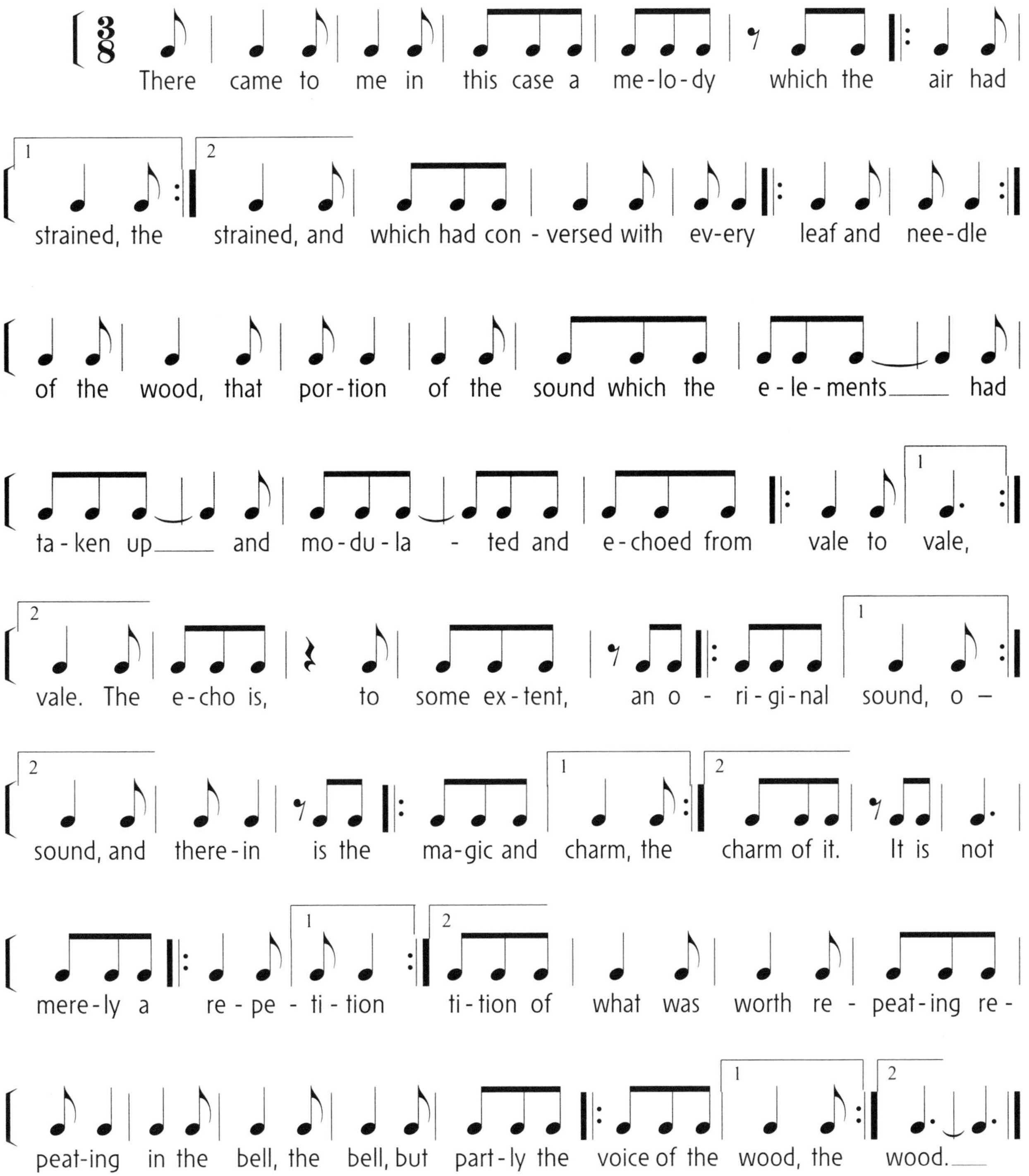

6/8 Time

6/8 time has six beats in a measure, divided into two groups of three.
As always, the first beat of each group has a metric accent.

1. Slap/Tap/Tap/Clap/Tap/Tap a familiar 6/8 ditty:

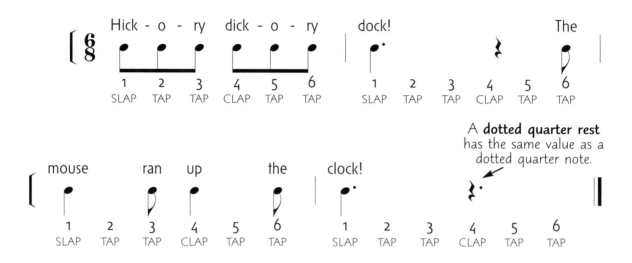

2. Like 3/8, 6/8 is often fast and reduces to two counts, on the metric accents. Slap/Clap it, leaving out the Taps:

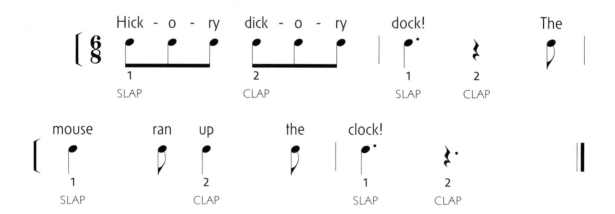

Stage-Fright

from *The New Home Speaker* (1911)

Frances Putnam Pogle

Joan Harkness

Apple Torte

Joan Harkness

Hemiola

Hemiola is a particular form of syncopation, in which the music alternately emphasizes metric accents and offbeats, creating a feeling of 3 against 2. As in other forms of syncopation, the effect is made by tying notes across the Great Divide between groups; in this case, groups of 3 beats.

In the little Talking Music, "Hey There," that follows, the first measure has notes on beats 1 and 4 (the two metric accents).

But the next measure puts notes on beats 1, 3, and 5 (the downbeat and two off-beats) *emphasizing beats 3 and 5 against* the metric accent of beat 4. You have to feel both the metric accents and the emphasis on the offbeats at once!

1. Slap/Clap/Tap it, repeating until you clearly feel the 3 against 2 rhythm:

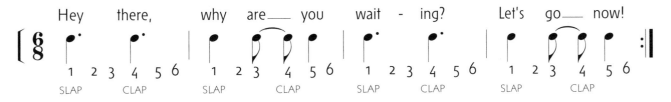

2. Do it again, leaving out the Taps, as you did with 6/8. Do it over and over until the swing of 3 against 2 feels easy and natural:

3. Sometimes the tied eighth notes are replaced by a quarter note. Try it:

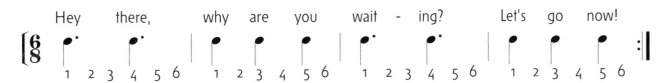

There's a wonderful book about composer John Cage by poet Joan Retallack called *Musicage: Cage muses on words, art, music*. During one interview, Ms. Retallack explains to Cage a game she plays with her university students to help them understand that intuition can be developed. Here's how it works: Give each person two pieces of paper. On the first piece of paper everyone writes a statement, something they know to be true. On the second piece of paper, everyone writes a question, something they really want to know. Gather the statements into one pile, and the questions into another. Then, beginning with the questions, read from the piles responsively, reading the statements as if they were the answers. And, usually, they are the answers! The questions and "answers" in this Talking Music are culled from the many times my family and friends have played this game at dinner parties.

Questions. Answers?

Joan Harkness

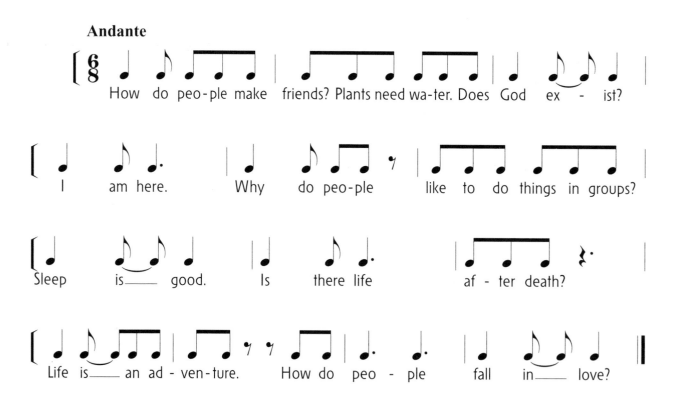

Improvisation

from The Life of Reason or the Phases of Human Progress: Reason in Art (1905)

George Santayana   Joan Harkness

sixteenth notes and rests have 2 flags

Sixteenth Notes and Rests

When you divide an eighth note in half, you get two sixteenth notes:
In music where the eighth note gets the beat, there are two sixteenths in one beat.

this is a
16th note
beam

1. As with eighth notes in 4 time, there's an "and" ("&") after each beat.
   Try it once counting "1 & 2 & 3 &," and again with the words:

2. Tie an eighth note to a sixteenth note:

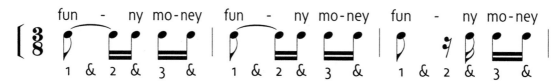

3. A **dotted eighth note** is the same as an eighth note tied to a sixteenth:

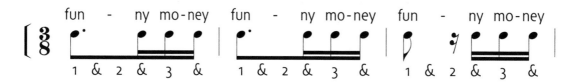

A 16th note beamed
to a eighth has a very
short **beam**

4. Here's a dotted eighth with the 16th note first:

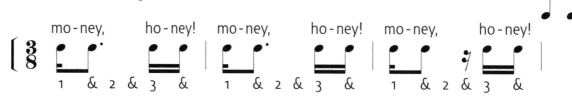

Mixed Seasons

Brains

from *The Wizard of Oz* (1900)

L. Frank Baum

Anna Dembska

"I have come for my brains," re-marked the Scare-crow, a lit-tle un-ea-si-ly. So the Wi-zard un-fas-tened his head. He took up a mea-sure of bran, which he mixed with a great man-y pins and nee-dles. He filled the top of the Scare-crow's head with the mix-ture and stuffed the rest of the space with straw, to hold it in place. Do-ro-thy looked at him cu-ri-ous-ly. His head was quite bulged out at the top with brains. "Why are those nee-dles and pins stick-ing out of your head?" asked the Tin Wood-man. "That is proof that he is sharp," re-marked the Li-on.

64

D.C. (Da Capo—i.e. "from the top") ***al Fine*** means: go back to the beginning and go on until you see ***Fine*** ("The End"), then stop.

The Ear

from *Gray's Anatomy* (1901)

Henry Gray, F. R. S.   Anna Dembska

The organ of hearing is divisible into three parts. The external ear consists of an expanded portion named auricle, and the auditory canal or meatus. The former serves to collect the vibrations by which the sound is produced; the latter conducts those vibrations to the tympanum. The middle ear, or tympanum, is an irregular cavity. The tympanum is traversed by a chain of movable bones, which serve to convey the vibrations communicated to the membrana tympani across the cavity of the tympanum to the inner ear. The internal ear is the essential part of the organ of hearing, receiving the ultimate distribution of the auditory nerve. It is called the labyrinth.

D.C. al Fine

9/8 time has three groups of three eighth notes. Slap/Clap/Tap it this way:

Or this way:

To Remove Fruit Stains

from "Helpful Hints to the Young Housekeeper,"
The Boston Cooking-School Cookbook, 1st Edition (1896)

Fannie Merrit Farmer

Anna Dembska

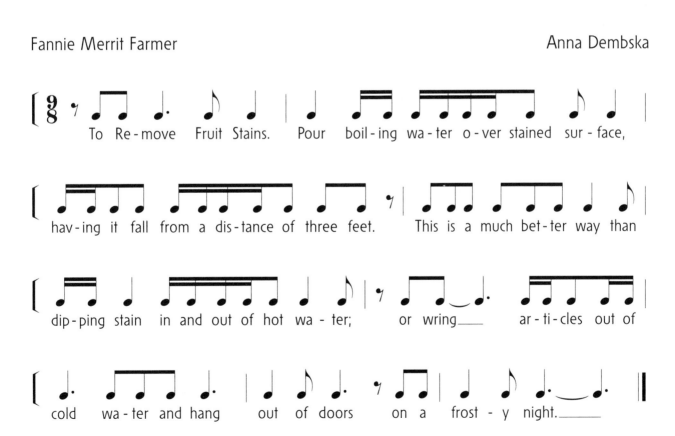

12/8 time has four groups of three beats. Try the Slap/Clap/Taps for 12/8:

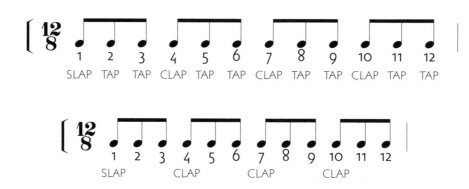

Opera Glasses at the Pawn Shop

from *Astronomy With an Opera-Glass* (1888)

Garrett P. Serviss

Joan Harkness

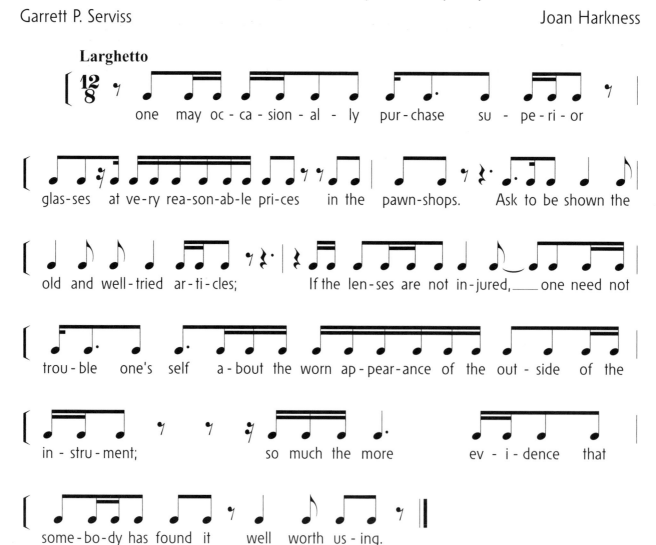

Syncopation Between the Beats

In 4/4, 3/4, 2/4, and 2/2

Syncopation can happen between the beats, on the "&" 's.

Dividing a beat into four parts allows syncopation in even smaller increments.

Eighth Note Syncopation in 4/4 Time

In 4/4 time, syncopation between the beats happens on eighth notes.
This type of syncopation is found in ragtime and the blues.

   1. Slap/Clap/Tap the next example, then do it again, counting out loud instead of saying the words:

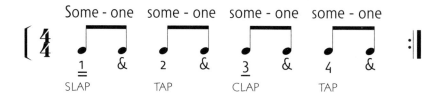

   2. In the next example, Slap/Clap/Tap and count again, but don't say "2" and "4" on beats 2 and 4. Listen to the syncopation that happens when there's a count on the "&" but not on the beat that follows. Then try it with the words. Repeat until you feel and hear the syncopation easily:

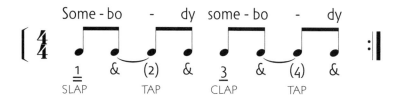

Often the tied eighth notes of syncopation are represented by a quarter note that comes between the beats. You'll especially see this notation in ragtime and jazz.

   3. Here's the same example substituting a quarter note for the tied eighth notes. Try it with the words, and then again counting without saying "2" and "4" on beats 2 and 4:

REMEMBER: As usual in music, you have to do at least two things at once: simultaneously feel the metric accents *and* the syncopated stresses!

Cheer

Work Song

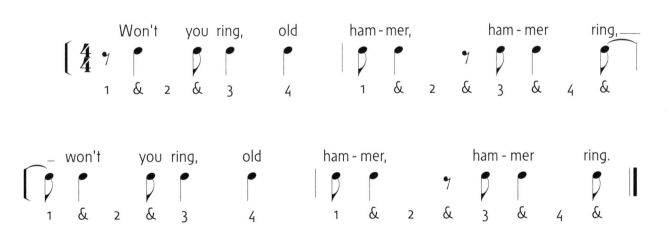

What Music Can Do

Isidore of Seville (d. 636)

Joan Harkness

Allegretto

Thus with-out mu-sic no dis-ci-pline can be

per-fect for there is no-thing with-out it. For the ve-ry

un-i-verse, it is said, is held to-ge-ther by a cer-tain har-

mo-ny of sounds, and the hea-vens them-selves are

made to re-volve by the mo-du-la-tion of har-mo-ny.

Mu-sic moves the feel-ings and chan-ges em-o-tions...

The ve-ry beasts al-so, ev-en ser-pents, birds, and dol-phins,

mu-sic in-cites to lis-ten to her me-lo-dy. But ev'-ry

word we speak, ev'-ry pul-sa-tion of our veins, is re-la-ted by

mu-si-cal rhy-thms to the pow-ers of har-mo-ny.

In this piece, the first line and a half is the refrain, followed by the verses. After each verse, **D.C.** (da capo) appears, so go back to the beginning and play the refrain again. ⊕ is the symbol for the **coda**, the section of music which ends a piece, also marked ⊕. **D.C al Coda** means "from the top to the coda." So go back to the beginning and when you reach the ⊕, jump to the coda, indicated by the second ⊕ (in the last staff), and continue to the end of the piece.

George Gershwin

Joan Harkness

Begin to slow down at the *ritardando* in the fourth line. As you gradually slow down, you'll reach the tempo of **meno mosso**, which means "less quickly." Go back to the original **allegro** when you see **a tempo**.

Storms Are Fine Speakers

from *The Mountains of California 1 (1894)*

John Muir

Joan Harkness

Four Notes in a Beat

A beat can be divided into four equal parts. In 4/4 time, there are four sixteenth notes in a beat.

1. Slap/Clap. Say "roll" on every beat:

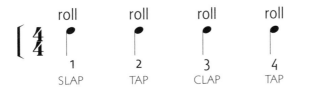

2. Now add the rest of "rollercoaster" in between each count. Slap/Clap/Tap is the same as in Step 1, but four notes now occupy each beat and sixteen notes occupy a measure, instead of four. Musicians say "1 ee & uh 2 ee & uh" to count a beat divided into four. Slap/Tap/Clap "rollercoaster" again, but count "1 ee & uh 2 ee & uh" out loud instead of saying "rollercoaster:"

3. Try these examples of mixed sixteenths and eighths:

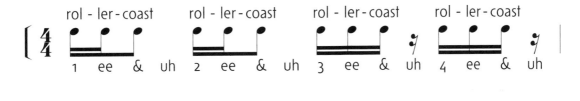

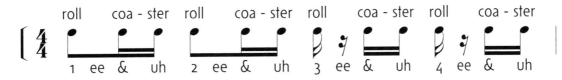

4. Sometimes a beam will cross rests between sixteenth and eighth notes. It looks different, but sounds the same as flagged notes with rests:

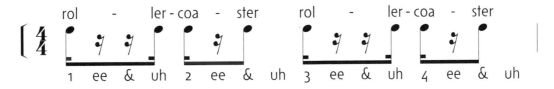

Suspending Disbelief

from *How To Tell Children Stories* (1915)

Sara Cone Bryant

Anna Dembska

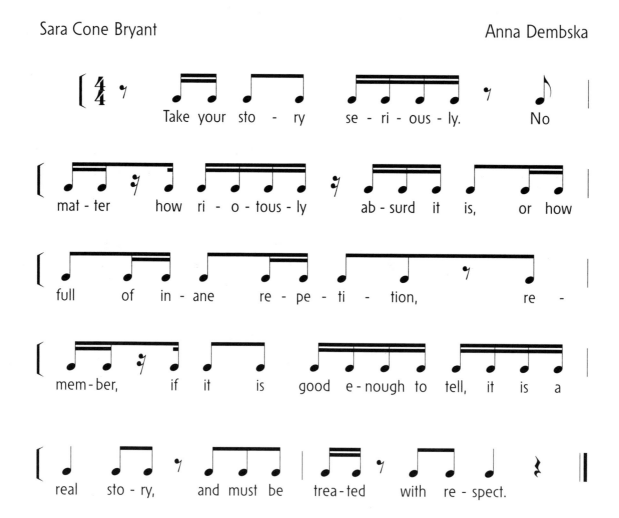

Take your sto - ry se - ri - ous - ly. No mat - ter how ri - o - tous - ly ab - surd it is, or how full of in - ane re - pe - ti - tion, re - mem - ber, if it is good e - nough to tell, it is a real sto - ry, and must be trea - ted with re - spect.

A couple of tips on pronouncing Spanish: the sound of a double "l" is equivalent to the sound of a "y", as in "yes" (see "Allende" and "Bellas"). A dipthong is the sound you'll make on the "io" of "Antonio" and "Revolución"." Pronounce the two vowels one right after another, sliding quickly between them, making a continuous sound.

Mexico City Metro

Joan Harkness

Variations on Four Notes in a Beat

1. Dotted eighths with sixteenths have the same relationship to each other in 4 time as in 8 time, but you'll count them differently. Say "roller" in the rhythm of a dotted eighth and a sixteenth, silently counting "1 ee & uh 2 ee & uh:"

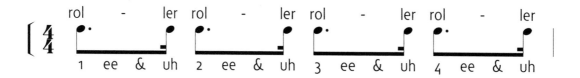

2. Try the opposite: a sixteenth followed by a dotted eighth. Keep counting silently:

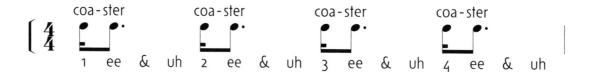

3. A dotted eighth rest is sometimes found with a sixteenth note:

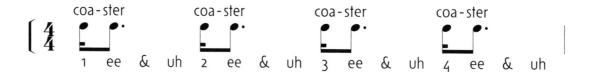

Reminds Me of Some Politicians

from *The Essays: "Of Vain-Glory,"* (1601)

Francis Bacon

Anna Dembska

The fly sat u-pon the a-xle-tree of the cha-ri-ot wheel, and said, "What a dust do I raise!" So are there some vain per-sons, that what-so-e-ver go-eth a-lone, or mo-veth u-pon grea-ter means, if they have ne-ver so lit-tle hand in it, they think it is they that car-ry it.

A Conversation

from *The Country of the Pointed Firs* (1896)

Sarah Orne Jewett

Anna Dembska

Sixteenth Note Syncopation

Sixteenth note syncopation is very common in ragtime music.

1. Slap/Clap/Tap this example, counting silently, repeating until it's effortless:

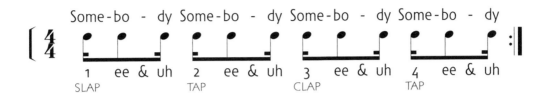

2. Syncopated notes can follow one after the other. Here's three in a row:

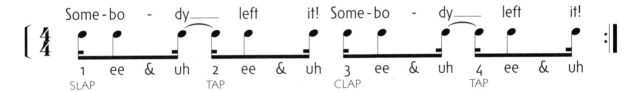

3. Try this example of sixteenth note syncopation followed by eighth note syncopation:

4. You may have noticed that you are counting more than one layer at once: the beats, with Slap/Tap/Clap/Tap, and the sixteenths, with the "1 ee & uh." With sixteenth note and eighth note syncopations in the same piece, it's sometimes useful to be able to shift to yet another count. In the next example, try shifting from "1 ee & uh 2 ee & uh" to "3 & 4 &."

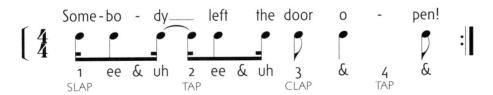

The sections of a piece of music are sometimes named by a letter, so you can easily understand its structure as a whole. The form of this piece is: Introduction AABBACCDD. The repeat signs and 1st and 2nd endings mark each section and its repeat.

The Ragtime King

Joan Harkness

8th Notes In 2/2 Time

There are two metric accents in 2/2 time. As you may remember, 2/2 time is like 4/4 time reduced to its metric accents. That's why you Slap and Clap instead of the Slap and Tap of 2/4 time. In 2 time, there are four eighth notes in one beat.

1. Count "1 ee & uh 2 ee & uh" out loud for eighth notes in 2/2 time. Then think the counts silently as you speak "rollercoaster:"

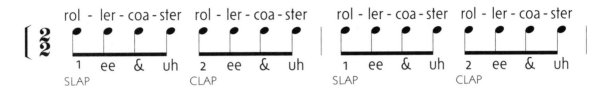

2. Try these examples of mixed quarters and eighths in 2/2 time:

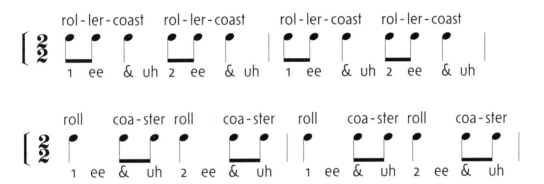

3. Dotted quarters with eighths in 2/2 are like dotted eighths and sixteeths in 2/4, 3/4 or 4/4. Say "roller" in the rhythm of a dotted quarter and an eighth, silently counting "1 ee & uh 2 ee & uh:"

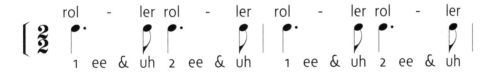

4. Try the opposite: a sixteenth followed by a dotted eighth. Keep counting silently:

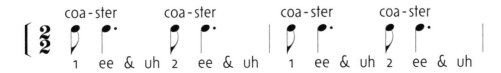

Sun-Treader

Joan Harkness

Eighth Note Syncopation In 2/2 Time

Eighth note syncopation in 2/2, or cut time, is counted like sixteenth note syncopation in 4 time.

1. Repeat the following examples, counting silently, until it's easy:

2. Try shifting your silent count from the "1 ee & uh 2 ee & uh" of eighth note syncopation to the "1 & 2 &" of quarter note syncopation:

An American Collaboration

Anna Dembska

Andante

Back in the nine-teen twen-ties, com-po-ser Vir-gil Thom-son met the wri-ter Ger-trude Stein in Pa-ris— at the time, the ar-tis-tic ca-pi-tol of the world. These two ec-cen-tric ar-tists wrote two u-nique ope-ras to-ge-ther: *Four Saints in Three Acts*— the long-est run-ning ope-ra e-ver on Broad-way, per-formed by an all-black cast and *The Mo-ther of Us All,* based on the life of Su-san B. An-tho-ny. Al-though they some-times quar-relled, this col-la-bo-ra-tion, with Stein's e-nig-ma-tic, re-pe-ti-tive text, and Thom-son's wit-ty and e-le-gant e-vo-ca-tion of mu-si-cal A-me-ri-ca-na, cre-a-ted a de-light-ful,__ tru-ly A-me-ri-can, an-ti-nar-ra-tive ope-ra!

Tuplets, Double Dots, Suspending the Meter, and No Meter

Triplets, Duples, Odd Tuplets, and Out of Time

When a beat or a note is divided into a number of equal parts, different from the normal divisions of a note in that meter, it's called a tuplet.

Sometimes a meter will be temporarily suspended. And sometimes, a score will have no meter at all.

Eighth Note Triplets

A **triplet** is a note divided into three equal parts. Eighth note triplets are made of three eighth notes with a "3" above or below them.

It's like three eighth notes squeezed into the duration of two eighth notes. You may also have triplets with a quarter note bracketed with an eighth note in the duration of two eighth notes (also the value of a quarter note!):

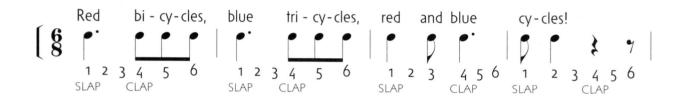

1. Do this 6/8 Talking Music, using only the Slap and Clap, and leaving out the Taps. Count the beats silently as you speak the words:

Red   bi - cy - cles,   blue   tri - cy - cles,   red   and blue   cy - cles!

2. Now we'll perform a musical magic trick that looks like this:

It means that the duration of a *dotted quarter note* in the previous example will now be the duration of a *quarter note* in the 2/4 example that follows. Your Slap/Clap will become a Slap/Tap, but their tempo will remain the same. The three eighth notes in the 6/8 example have been transformed into a triplet which lasts the duration of one quarter note (two eighth notes) in 2/4 time. Eighth note triplets in 2/4, 3/4 and 4/4 times (referred to in this book as "4 time") are counted "1 & uh 2 & uh." Silently count as you do this 2/4 example:

Red   bi - cy - cles,   blue   tri - cy - cles,   red   and blue   cy - cles!

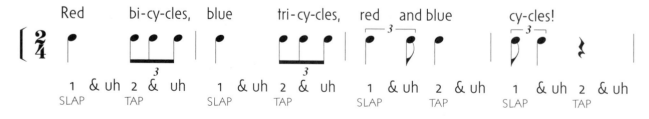

3. Let's go back to plain old 2/4 eighth notes and remember what it feels like to divide a note into two equal parts. You'll be counting "1 & 2 &" silently. Repeat the following example until it's embedded in your brain:

4. Now try counting out loud, moving back and forth between triplet counting and normal eighth counting. Keep your Slap/Tap steady. Notice that the only time you'll count "1 & uh 2 & uh" is when you're actually in the midst of a triplet. Repeat until it's easy to switch back and forth:

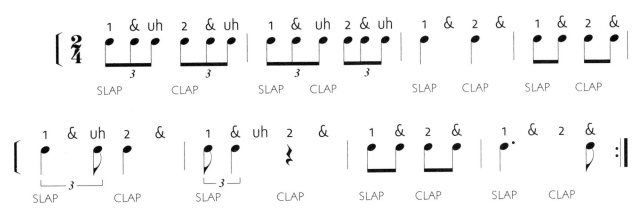

5. For the grand finale, try all the bicycles together. Repeat the first line until it's easy, then go on the the second:

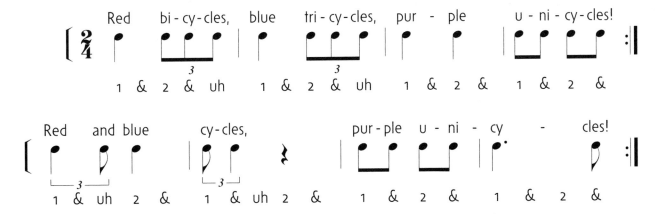

Try these little triplet Talking Musics inspired by words found on the refrigerator:

Magnetic Poetry 4

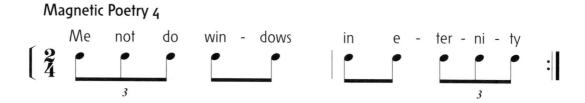

Magnetic Poetry 5

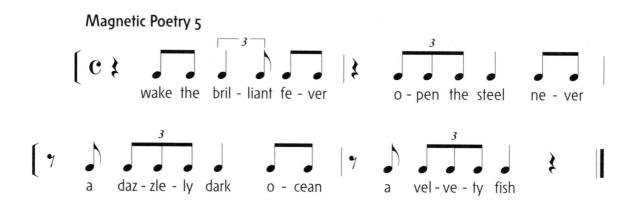

Random Salad

Johannes Kepler as quoted in *Astronomy with an Opera-Glass* (1888)

Garrett P. Serviss   Joan Harkness

Yes-ter-day, when I was wea-ry with wri-ting, my mind be-ing quite dus-ty with con-si-der-ing these a-toms, I was called to sup-per, and a sa-lad I had asked for was set be-fore me. "It seems, then," said I, a-loud, "that if pew-ter di-shes, leaves of let-tuce, grains of salt, drops of wa-ter, vi-ne-gar and oil, and sli-ces of egg, had been fly-ing a-bout in the air from all e-ter-ni-ty, it might at last hap-pen by chance that there would come a sa-lad." "Yes," says my wife, "but not so nice and well-dressed as this of mine is."

The ***D. S. al Fine*** (***Dal Segno al Fine***) at the end of this piece means "from the sign to the end." When you come to ***D. S. al Fine***, go back to the sign: 𝄋 and continue to ***Fine*** ("end"), and stop there.

Crimped Crust Quaker Bread

Advertisement from *The Boston Cooking-School Cookbook*, 1st edition (1896)

Anna Dembska

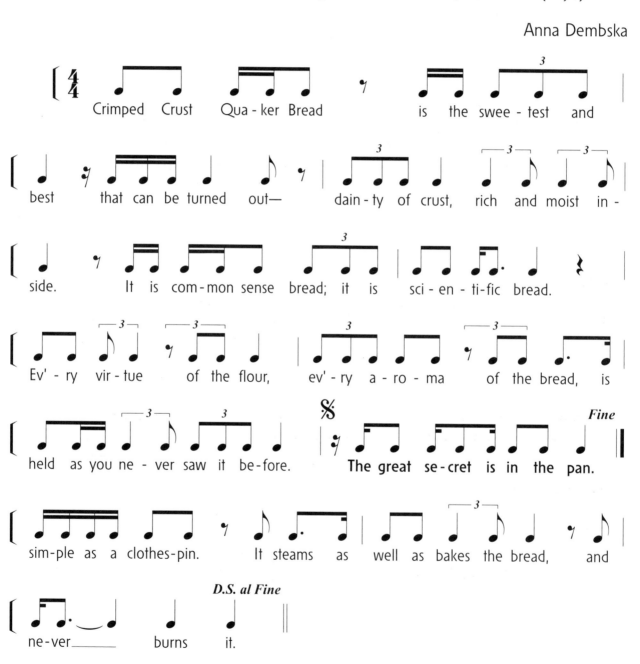

Double Dots 𝅗𝅥..

With one dot after a note, as you know, the value is increased by one-half. With *two* dots, the value is increased again by one-half of the first dot (in other words, a quarter of the original note). In 4 time:

$$
\begin{array}{ll}
\text{♩} = 1 & \text{𝅗𝅥} = 2 \\
+ \text{ .} = 1/2 & + \text{ .} = 1 \\
\underline{+ \text{ .} = 1/4} & \underline{+ \text{ .} = 1/2} \\
\text{♩.. } = 1\ 3/4 & \text{𝅗𝅥.. } = 3\ 1/2
\end{array}
$$

1. Since a quarter of a beat—the value of a sixteenth note—is the smallest common denominator in a double-dotted quarter note, count "1 ee & uh" as you do with sixteenth notes. In fact, you'll almost always find a double dotted quarter note paired with a sixteenth note:

A Victorian Admonition

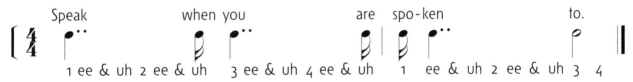

2. With a dotted half note, which usually pairs with an eighth note, count in eighths ("1 & 2 & 3 & 4 &"), the lowest common denominator:

Temperature Rising

The Dispute

from *Pigs is Pigs* (1906)

Ellis Parker Butler

Anna Dembska

Mike Flan-ne-ry leaned o-ver the coun-ter of the ex-press of-fice and shook his fist. Mis-ter More-house, an-gry and red, stood on the o-ther side of the coun-ter, trem-bling with rage. The cause of the trou-ble stood on the coun-ter be-tween the two men. It was a soap box a-cross the top of which were nailed a num-ber of strips, for-ming a rough but ser-vice-a-ble cage. In it two spot-ted gui-nea-pigs were gree-di-ly ea-ting let-tuce leaves.

The Hatter and Alice

from *Alice in Wonderland* (1862)

Lewis Carroll

Joan Harkness

A-lice sighed wea-ri-ly. "I think you might do some-thing bet-ter with the time,"

she said, "than wast-ing it in as-king rid-dles that have no an-swers."

"If you knew Time as well as I do," said the Hat-ter, "you

would-n't talk____ a-bout wast-ing it. It's him." "I

don't know what you mean," said A-lice. "Of course you don't!" the Hat-ter said. "I

dare say you ne-ver e-ven spoke to Time!" "Per-haps not," A-lice

cau-tious-ly re-plied; "but I know I have to beat time when I learn mu-sic."

"Ah! That ac-counts for it," said the Hat-ter. "He won't stand beat-ing."

Quarter Note Triplets

Three quarter note triplets are the same duration as a half note:

1. To count quarter note triplets, we'll detour back to hemiola in 6/8 time. Slap/Clap this
   example again, to remember the swing of hemiola.

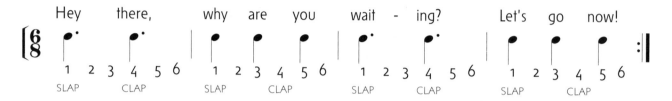

2. Now switch to 2/4 time and let
   Count "1 & uh 2 & uh." Feel the syncopation falling on the "uh" and the "&":

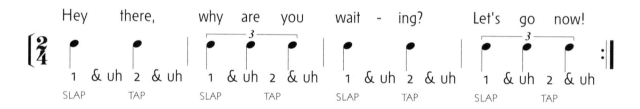

3. This time, count "1 & 2 &" for the regular quarter notes, and "1 & uh 2 & uh" for the
   triplets, keeping your Slap/Tap steady.

4. Try an example with some eighth notes:

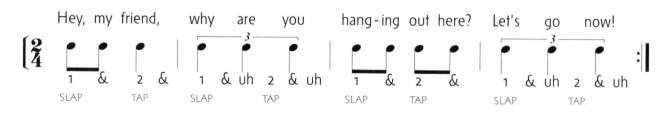

Radish

from *Burpee's Farm Annual 1888*

Joan Harkness

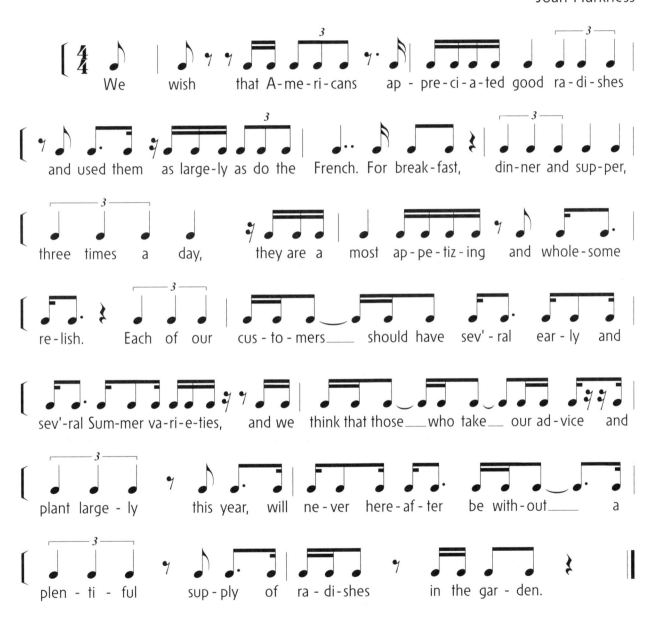

We wish that A-me-ri-cans ap-pre-ci-a-ted good ra-di-shes
and used them as large-ly as do the French. For break-fast, din-ner and sup-per,
three times a day, they are a most ap-pe-tiz-ing and whole-some
re-lish. Each of our cus-to-mers___ should have sev'-ral ear-ly and
sev'-ral Sum-mer va-ri-e-ties, and we think that those___who take___ our ad-vice and
plant large-ly this year, will ne-ver here-af-ter be with-out___ a
plen-ti-ful sup-ply of ra-di-shes in the gar-den.

Duples in Compound Meter

Duples are the opposite of triplets: there are two notes in the space of three notes. You'll find quarter-note duples replacing three eighth notes (or a dotted quarter note, or a quarter and an eighth note) in 8 time (3/8, 6/8, 9/8, 12/8, etc.):

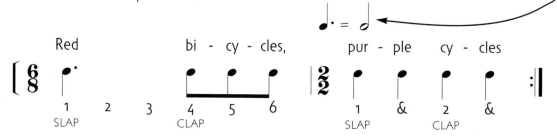

1. In the following example, the time signature changes from 6/8 to 2/2. This marking above the staff tells you that the Slap/Clap pulse stays steady as you move from 6/8 to 2/2. But you need to change the count from the 3 divisions of the pulse in 6/8, to the two divisions of the pulse in 2/2 time.

2. The second measure of this example stays in 6/8 time, and the quarter notes transform into quarter note duples. It sounds exactly the same as the previous example. In the second line of music, notice the difference in your internal counting between the quarter/eighth-note combination, and the quarter-note duple. Practice each line until you can switch the count effortlessly.

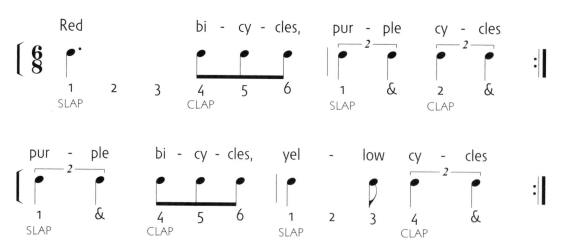

Insinuating Rhythm

from *The Life of Reason or the Phases of Human Progress: Reason in Art* (1905)

George Santayana   Joan Harkness

Odd Tuplets

Sometimes you'll see groups of notes that look like triplets or duples, but have a 5, 6, 7, or other number above them instead of a 2 or 3. Any such group, including triplets and duples, is called a **tuplet**. And just as with triplets or duples, the total value is evenly divided among all the notes in a tuplet. With these larger, usually rapid, tuplet groups, there's no easy way to count out the values. Instead, keep your Slap/Clap/Tap steady, keep the duration of the beat in your mind, and fit the tuplets into the beat as evenly as possible.

1. A sixteenth note tuplet of 5 (a **quintuplet**) squeezes five sixteenth notes into the space of a quarter note:

Resignation

Once you're in a long line,   there's no-thing to do but   wait.

2. A sixteenth note tuplet of six (a **sextuplet**) fits six sixteenth notes into the space of a quarter note:

Points of View

Up - side down Right - side up Back - ward   and   For - ward

3. A sixteenth note tuplet of seven (a **septuplet**) squeezes seven sixteenth notes into the duration of a quarter note:

Your Choice

If you like it that way then do   it   your   way!

Pickles, Relishes and Sauces

from the *Madison County* (Nebraska) *1998 Open Class Fairbook*

Joan Harkness

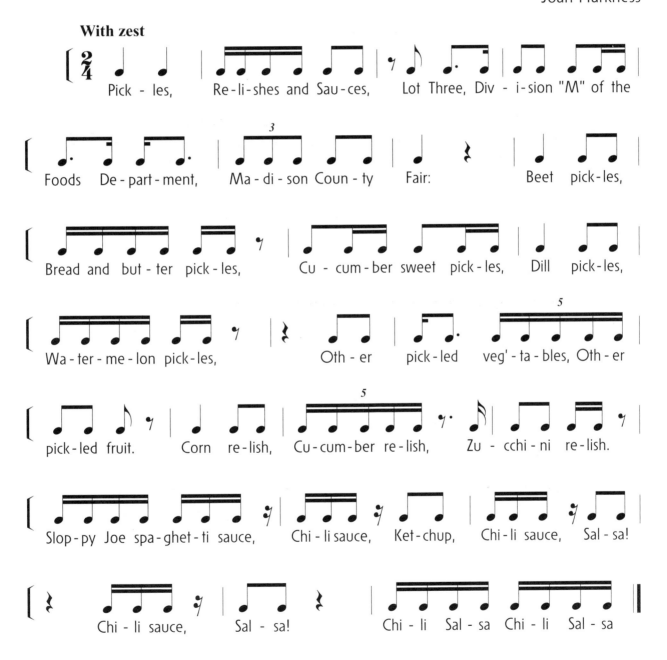

Plants

from U.S. Fish and Wildlife Service website, Division of Endangered Species, Region 5

Joan Harkness

Suspending the Meter, and the Breve

A **breve** is twice as long as a whole note: 8 beats in 4 time; 4 beats in 2 time. But sometimes a breve is used to indicate chanting many words on a single note, **out of time** (freely, ignoring the meter), as in "A Style of Reading," below.

Hold the Slap in the breve measures, take as long as you need to speak all the words, and resume your 4/4 Slap/Tap/Clap/Tap in the next bar.

A Style of Reading

from *The New Home Speaker* (1911)

Frances Putnam Pogle   Joan Harkness

No Meter

This piece has no meter! Composers sometimes do this, for a variety of reasons. In this case, the metric feeling follows the rhythm of the words. Use a quarter note as the beat, Slapping on each one.

How To Sit

from *The New Home Speaker* (1911)

Frances Putnam Pogle

Joan Harkness

Irregular and Shifting Meters

5/8, 5/4, 7/8, 10/8, 6/8 + 3/4, 2/4 + 5/8, etc.

Irregular meters combine groups of two beats with groups of three beats.

In some compositons with changing meters, the value of the beat itself may change, shifting from 6/8 to 3/4 to 7/8 to...?

5/8 Time

We now come to a new kind of meter: **irregular**. The meters you've encountered so far have been made of groups of two beats or groups of three beats. Irregular meters combine groups of two beats with groups of three beats.

The simplest of these irregular meters is 5/8. It has one group of two beats and one group of three beats. As always, the downbeat has a metric accent. But the position of the other metric accent can change, depending on which group comes first—the two-beat or the three-beat.

1. Here's the 2 + 3 5/8 meter. Count the beats aloud as you Slap/Clap/Tap:

2. Now count and Slap/Clap/Tap the 3 + 2 5/8 meter:

Notice how the beams help you to see how the meter is divided. Sometimes, to assist you further, a composer will actually spell out the divisions in the time signature like this:

$$\frac{5}{8}(2+3)$$

But often, you have to figure it out for yourself. In the pieces that follow, investigate the groupings of beats before you begin. The beaming will provide clues. Counting one for nothing before the beginning of a piece is especially important with irregularly-metered music, so that you're clear about the position of the metric accents before you start.

It's always possible, of course, that a composer will change groupings in the middle of a piece. Constant vigilance is advised!

Doctor's Orders

from *The Compleat Gentleman* (1622)

Henry Peacham   Joan Harkness

Vivace

The phy-si-cians will tell you that the ex-er-cise of mu-sic is a

great length-en-er of the life by stir-ring and re-vi-

ving of the spi-rits hol-ding a se-cret sym-pa-thy

with them. So said Hen-ry Peach-am in *The Com-pleat Gen-tle-*

man, pub-lished in the year six-teen twen-ty two.

Chávez

Joan Harkness

5/4 Time

5/4 time is similar to 5/8 time.

Count and Slap/Clap/Tap the two different metric accentings of 5/4:

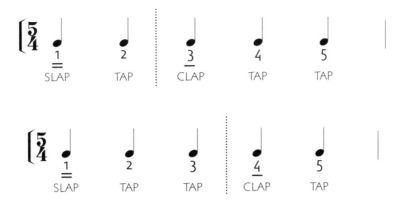

It's harder to recognize the note groupings (and thus the metric accents) than with 5/8 time, because you don't have the beaming to clue you in. But here are some other hints to look for:

1. The placement of larger notes:

   In the first full measure of "Mother Theophila Says..." notice the dotted quarter and eighth notes followed by a half and a quarter note. The Great Divide between the groups would be between the eighth and the half, since the half and the quarter add up to three. The last bar shows the Divide even more clearly.

2. The way notes are tied:

   Ties cross the Great Divide between groups of two and three notes, as described with 4/4 measures back at the beginning of this book. In the second full bar of "Mother Theophila Says...," there's a tie between beats 2 and 3, indicating the Divide between a two-beat group followed by a three-beat group.

Mother Theophila Says...

Rewards

from *Rhythm, Music, and Education* (1921)

Emile Jaques-Dalcroze   Joan Harkness

Andante

Once ar-rived at our des-ti-na-tion, what mat-ters the time we have ta-ken! The es-sen-tial is that we should have been ab-le to make the jour-ney, and have known where we were go-ing.... Joy is at-tained with the first step towards pro-gress. Thence-for-ward, it will in-ten-si-fy un-ceas-ing-ly; ren-der-ing us ca-pa-ble of the high-est and most un-ex-pec-ted ach-ieve-ments. Fin-al-ly, com-bin-ing with our sub-con-scious for-ces, it will take firm root, fol-low-ing the in-ev-it-a-ble law of life, bring forth buds and fruits and flo-wers.

7/8 Time

7/8 time consists of two groups of two and one group of three. There are three possible groupings: 3 + 2 + 2, 2 + 2 + 3, and 2 + 3 + 2.

Count out loud as you Slap/Tap/Clap. Notice how the feeling changes with different metric accents:

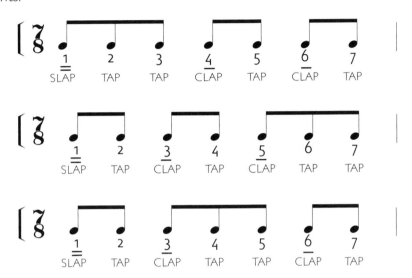

Percussion

Joan Harkness

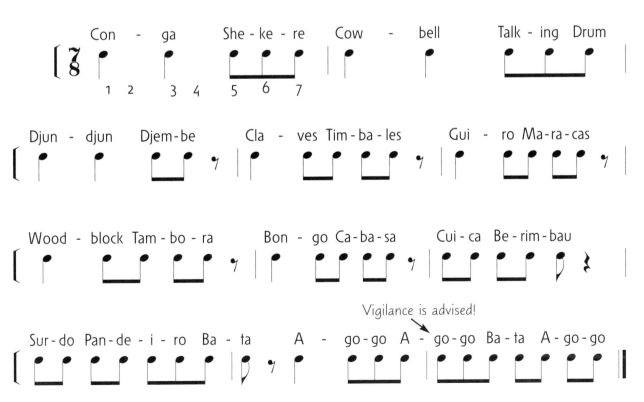

Vigilance is advised!

Harry Partch

Anna Dembska

Bartók

Joan Harkness

10/8 Time

As you may imagine, 10/8 time can be divided into numerous and varied groupings of twos and threes. Right now we'll delve into this one: 3 + 3 + 2 + 2:

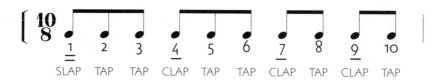

Thanksgiving Day

Joan Harkness

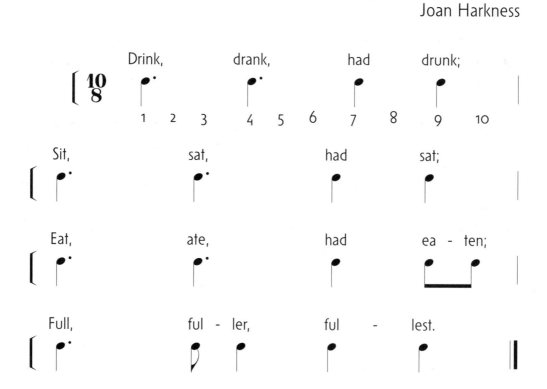

Astronomy With an Opera-Glass

from *Astronomy With an Opera-Glass* (1888)

Garritt P. Serviss

Joan Harkness

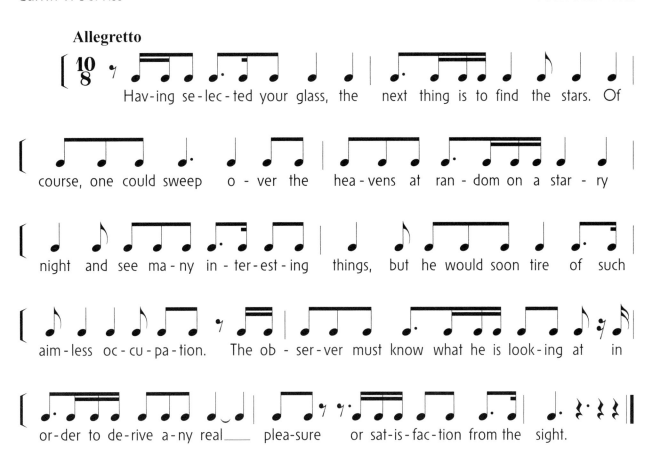

Shifting Meters

You've practiced many pieces with meter changes. But when the value of the beat (the bottom numbers of the time signatures) changes in the middle of a piece, things get a bit more complicated. You need to count in your head at the lowest common denominator—in the following examples, the eighth note.

The eighth notes in 6/8 time and 3/4 time all have the same duration. But the Slap/Tap/Tap/Clap/Tap/Tap of 6/8 time will be twice as fast as the Slap/Clap/Tap of 3/4. This particular meter change between 6/8 and 3/4 is another way of notating hemiola.

1. Do this piece really slowly until it's perfectly clear what's going on. Then try the 6/8 bars leaving out the Taps, and feel 6/8 with its two metric accents against the three metric accents of 3/4:

Jurassic Park

2. Try shifting between 7/8 and 4/4. Make sure you know before you start which 7/8 Slap/Clap/Tap pattern you'll be using:

Rationalization

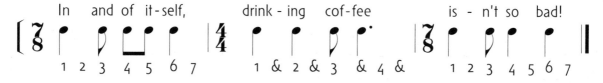

Aaron Copland

Joan Harkness

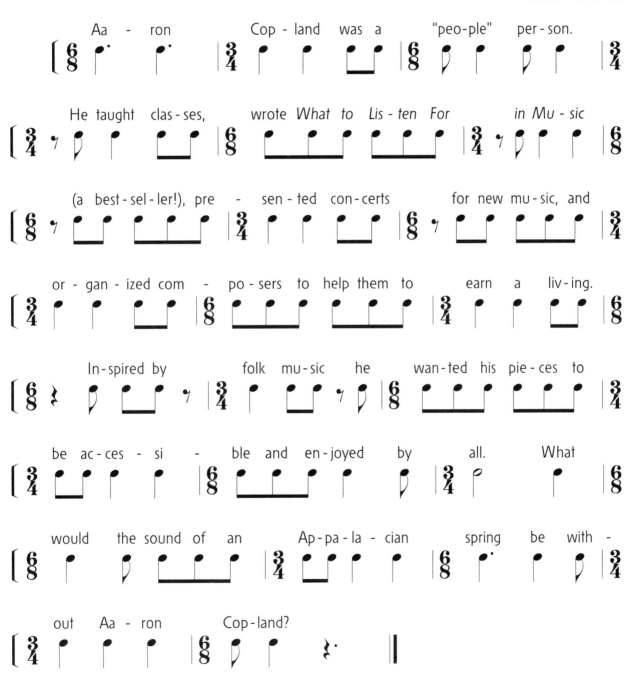

Stravinsky

Joan Harkness

Agitato

Bar - ba - ric! Pri - mi - tive! An out - rage! *The*

Rite of Spring (a bal - let) by Ig - or Stra - vin - sky pro - voked a

ri - ot in Pa - ris at its first per - for - mance. Rhy - thms

that ig - nored___ the rules: a diff' - rent me - ter ev' - ry

bar, ac - cents on un - sus - pect - ing beats. Un - re - lent - ing

pow - er - ful sounds and or - ches - tral ef - fects ex - plo - ded the

boun - da - ries of mu - sic. The year was nine - teen - thir -

teen and it must have seemed to con - cert - go - ers that the mo - dern

mu - si - cal sen - sa - tions of the new cen - tu - ry had be - gun!

Practice

Anna Dembska

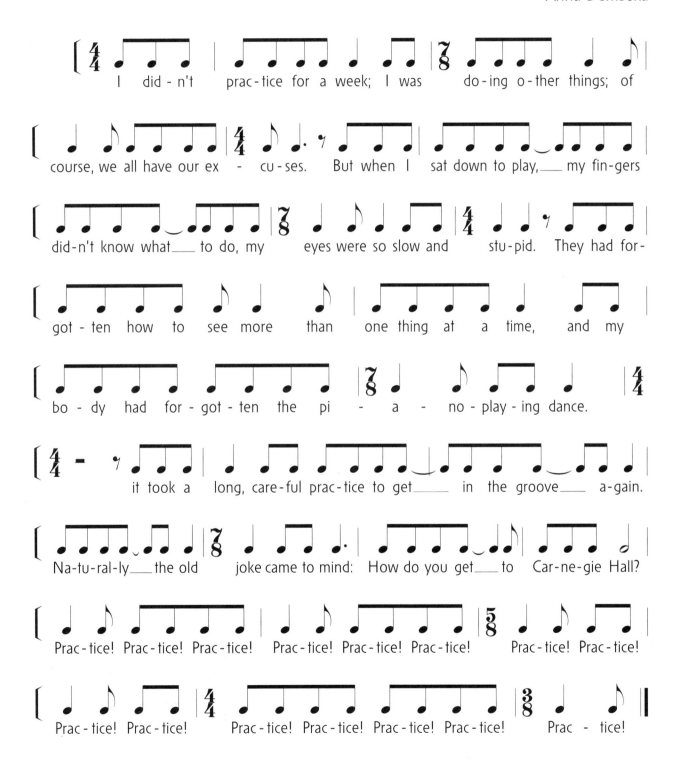

I did-n't prac-tice for a week; I was do-ing o-ther things; of course, we all have our ex - cu-ses. But when I sat down to play,＿ my fin-gers did-n't know what＿ to do, my eyes were so slow and stu-pid. They had for-got-ten how to see more than one thing at a time, and my bo-dy had for-got-ten the pi - a - no-play-ing dance. it took a long, care-ful prac-tice to get＿ in the groove＿ a-gain. Na-tu-ral-ly＿ the old joke came to mind: How do you get＿ to Car-ne-gie Hall? Prac-tice! Prac-tice! Prac-tice! Prac-tice! Prac-tice! Prac-tice! Prac-tice! Prac-tice! Prac-tice! Prac-tice! Prac-tice! Prac-tice! Prac-tice! Prac-tice! Prac - tice!

Advice From a Caterpillar

from *Alice in Wonderland* (1862)

Lewis Carroll   Anna Dembska

"What size do you want to be?" it asked. "Oh, I'm not par-ti-cu-lar as to size," A-lice has-ti-ly re-plied, "on-ly one does-n't like chang-ing so of-ten you know." "I don't know," said the ca-ter-pil-ler.

The Tempo Page

Tempo, the Italian word for time, is the speed at which a piece is performed. Sometimes the tempo of a piece of music will change, in which case, the composer will make a new tempo marking at the moment of change. The traditional tempo markings are in Italian, but composers often describe tempos in their own languages. Here are some traditional tempo markings, from slowest to fastest:

Grave . . . . .slow, solemn

Largo . . . . .large, broad, very slow, stately

Larghetto . . . ."a little largo," i.e. slightly faster than largo

Adagio . . . . .slow, leisurely

Lento . . . . .slow

Andante . . . ."going," or "walking," moderately slow

Moderato . . . . .moderate

Allegretto . . . . .a little allegro, i.e. fairly fast

Allegro . . . ."cheerful," fast

Vivace . . . . .lively, quick

Presto . . . . .very fast

Prestissimo . . . . .as fast as possible

There are also tempo markings for changing the tempo:

***Ritardando**, (**rit.** or **ritard.**)* . . . . .gradually slow down

***Rallentando**, (**rall.**)* . . . . gradually slow down

***Accelerando**, (**accel.**)* . . . . accelerate, or gradually speed up

A tempo, used after ***rit.**, **rall.**,* and ***accel***. . . . . resume the previous tempo

🎵 , or **fermata** (Italian for "pause"). . . . . hold the note longer than its value

meno mosso . . . . less quickly

Partial Bibliograpy for Composers

Here's a selective, personal bibliography for the artists who are subjects of Talking Music pieces. We'll be adding more information and links about these composers at our web site: http://www.fleap.com.

Béla Bartók (1881-1945)

RECORDINGS: Many recordings are available of Bartók's music, such as *Concerto for Orchestra, Sonata for Two Pianos and Percussion, Mikrokosmos* for piano.

John Cage (1912-1992)

RECORDINGS: *The Perilous Night* and *Four Walls.* Margaret Leng Tan, pianist and Joan La Barbara, soprano. New Albion 37.

Sonatas and Interludes. Maro Ajemian, prepared piano. Composers Recordings Inc. CRI 700.

PUBLICATIONS: Cage, John. *Musicage: Cage Muses on Words, Art, Music.* Edited by Joan Retallack. Wesleyan University Press, 1995.

Cage, John. *Silence.* Wesleyan University Press, 1961.

Revill, David. *The Roaring Silence: John Cage: A Life.* Arcade Publishers, 1992.

VIDEO: *Cage/Cunningham.* A documentary film from 1995.

Carlos Chávez (1899-1978)

RECORDINGS: *Latin American Ballets.* Eduardo Mata conducts the Simón Bolívar Symphony Orchestra. Dorian 90211.

The Complete Symphonies. Eduardo Mata conducts the London Symphony Orchestra. Vox Box 5061.

PUBLICATIONS: Parker, Robert L. *Carlos Chávez: Mexico's Modern-Day Orpheus.* Twayne Publishers, 1983.

Aaron Copland (1900-1990)

RECORDINGS: In addition to *Appalachian Spring*, Copland's famous works for orchestra include *Billy the Kid* and the *Symphony No. 3.*

PUBLICATIONS: Copland, Aaron, and Vivian Perlis. *Copland 1900 Through 1942.* St. Martin's/Marek, reprint edition, 1999.

Copland, Aaron, and Vivian Perlis. *Copland Since 1943.* St. Martin's/Marek, reprint edition, 1999.

Copland, Aaron. *What to Listen for in Music.* Penguin USA paperback, reprint edition, 1999.

George Gershwin (1898-1937)

RECORDINGS: Many of the songs George Gershwin wrote with his brother Ira are now jazz standards. The opera *Porgy and Bess, An American In Paris* and *Rhapsody in Blue* for orchestra, and the *Preludes* for solo piano are widely available on recordings and are often performed in concert.

Charles Ives (1874-1954)

RECORDINGS: *The Complete Songs of Charles Ives*. Steven Blier, piano, William Sharp, baritone, and Dora Ohrenstein, soprano, among others. Albany Records 77-80.

Three Places in New England. David Zinman conducts the Baltimore Symphony Orchestra, Baltimore Symphony Chorus. Argo 44860.

PUBLICATIONS: Perlis, Vivian. *Charles Ives Remembered: An Oral History*. Yale University Press, 1974.

Swafford, Jan. *Charles Ives: A Life with Music*. W.W. Norton, 1996.

Scott Joplin (1868-1917)

RECORDINGS: Joplin's piano rags are widely available on compact disc. He also wrote an opera:

Treemonisha. Original cast recording. Gunther Schuller, conductor, with Betty Allen, Carmen Balthrop, and the Houston Grand Opera Chorus and Orchestra. Deutsche Grammophon 35709.

Mary Jane Leach

RECORDINGS: *Ariadne's Lament*. Featuring conductors Virginia Davidson and William Payn; performers Jennifer Leshnower, Kelley Mikkelsen, the Cassatt String Quartet, and the New York Treble Singers. New World Records 80525.

Celestial Fires. New York Treble Singers, conducted by Virginia Davidson; Shannon Peet, bassoon; Mary Jane Leach, voice; and Barbara Held, alto flute. XI Records 107. Available at CDEMusic.org and forcedexposure.com.

Pauline Oliveros

RECORDINGS: *Deep Listening*. Pauline Oliveros, Stuart Dempster, and Panaiotis. New Albion Records 022.

PUBLICATIONS: Oliveros, Pauline. *Software for People: Collected Writings 1963-1980*. 1983. Available from the *Deep Listening™ Catalog*.

The annotated Deep Listening™ Catalog, Pauline Oliveros Foundation, Inc., P.O. Box 1956, Kingston, NY 12402

Harry Partch (1901-1974)

RECORDINGS: *The Harry Partch Collection.* Recordings supervised by the composer. Composers Recordings, Inc. CRI 751-754.

MULTI-MEDIA: *Enclosures.* "A multi-media portrait of the unconventional life of Harry Partch," directed by Dr. Philip Blackburn. Innova Recordings, the 400 Series.

VIDEO: *The Dreamer That Remains: A Study in Loving.* A documentary film directed by Stephen Poulliot. Available from Composers Recordings, Inc.

Terry Riley

RECORDINGS: Terry Riley is one of the fathers of minimalist music, and has many recordings available. Several versions of *In C* are available, including New Albion 71 and Sony Classics 7178.

Carl Ruggles (1876-1971)

RECORDINGS: *Sun-treader.* Christoph von Dohnányi conducts the Cleveland Orchestra. London Classics 443776.

Igor Stravinsky (1882-1971)

RECORDINGS: Many recordings are available of Stravinsky's works. For orchestra, *Le Sacre du Printemps* (The Rite of Spring) and *Petrushka* are well-known. A chorus accompanied by four pianos and percussion performs *Les Noces* (The Wedding). *L'Histoire du Soldat* (The Soldier's Tale) is a dramatic work for chamber ensemble.

Virgil Thomson (1896-1989) and Gertrude Stein (1874-1946)

RECORDINGS: *The Mother of Us All.* With Raymond Leppard, conductor, and the Santa Fe Opera Chorus, Santa Fe Opera Orchestra. New World Records 288.

Four Saints in Three Acts. Virgil Thomson and Leopold Stokowski conduct the Hollywood Bowl Symphony Orchestra in a recording from 1947. BMG/RCA Victor 68163.

VIDEO: *Virgil Thomson At 90.* A documentary film produced and directed by John Huszar.

PUBLICATIONS: Watson, Steven. *Prepare for Saints: Gertrude Stein, Virgil Thomson, and the Mainstreaming of American Modernism.* Random House, 1999.

General

PUBLICATIONS: Chase, Gilbert. *America's Music: From the Pilgrims to the Present.* 3rd ed. University of Illinois Press, 1987.

Delio, Thomas. *Circumscribing the Open Universe: Essays on John Cage, Morton Feldman, Christian Wolff, Robert Ashley, Alvin Lucier.* University Press of America, 1984.

Duckworth, William. *Talking Music: Conversations With John Cage, Philip Glass, Laurie Anderson, and Five Generations of American Experimental Composers.* Schirmer Books, 1995.

General (cont.)

Gagne, Cole, Gene Bagnato, and Lona Foote. *Soundpieces 1* and *Soundpieces 2: Interviews With American Composers*. Scarecrow Press, 1993. These are currently out of print, but available in some libraries.

Hitchcock, H. Wiley. *Music in the United States: A Historical Introduction*. 2nd ed. Prentice-Hall, 1974.

Kirkpatrick, John, Andrea Olmstead, and Bruce Saylor. *Twentieth-Century American Masters: Ives, Thomson, Sessions, Cowell, Gershwin, Copland, Carter, Barber, Cage, Bernstein*. Reprint edition. W. W. Norton, 1997.

Rich, Alan. *American Pioneers: Ives to Cage and Beyond*. Phaidon Press Inc., 1995.

Rockwell, John. *All American Music: Composition in the Late Twentieth Century*. Da Capo Press, 1997.

Southern, Eileen. *The Music of Black Americans: A History*. 3rd ed. W.W. Norton, 1997.

Strickland, Edward. *American Composers: Dialogues on Contemporary Music*. Indiana Univ. Press, 1991.

Sumner, Melody, Kathleen Burch, and Michael Sumner. *The Guests Go in to Supper: John Cage, Robert Ashley, Yoko Ono, Laurie Anderson, Charles Amirkhanian, Michael Peppe, K. Atchley*. Burning Books, 1986. This book is not in print, but may be available in some libraries.

VIDEO: *4 American Composers*. Four films about composers Meredith Monk, Robert Ashley, John Cage, and Philip Glass. 1999. These films are not in print, but may be available in libraries or at video rental stores.

Audible Laundry: The Music of Sound. A documentary film by Andrea Hawks, featuring Anna Dembska, soprano and Joan Harkness, piano. 1996. Available from Flying Leap Music.

Glossary with 3-Volume Index

The page where the term is explained follows the definition.

---

anacrusis. A pickup. p. 24

bar. A measure. p. 8

bar lines. The vertical lines that divide measures from each other. p. 8

beam. A line which connects notes which would otherwise have flags. By replacing the flags and connecting the notes, beams show how the notes are metrically grouped. p. 38

chorus. A refrain which repeats after each verse of a song. p. 36

coda. A section of music added on to end a piece. (See Da Capo al Coda) p. 71

common time. 4/4 time. p. 43

compound meter. A meter in which there are two or more pulses in a measure, with each pulse divided into three, such as 6/8, 9/8, or 12/8. p. 51

cut time. 2/2 time. p. 49

Da Capo al Coda (***D.C. al Coda***). Literally, "from the top to the coda." (See **coda**.) It indicates to go back to the beginning and when you reach the ⊕, jump to the coda (sometimes marked with a second ⊕), and continue to the end. p. 71

Da Capo al Fine (***D.C. al Fine***). Literally, "from the top to the end." It indicates to go back to the beginning and play on until you see ***Fine*** ("The End"), then stop. p. 64

Dal Segno al Fine (***D.S. al Fine***). Literally, "from the sign to the end." It indicates to go back to the sign, which looks like this: 𝄋 , and play until you get to ***Fine***, and end there. p. 90

dotted note. A note followed by a dot. A dot lengthens the duration of a note by half of the note's original value. A second dot lengthens the note by an additional half of a half (a quarter of the note's original value). p. 20, p. 91

downbeat. The first beat of a measure. It always has the strongest metric accent. p. 9

duple. The division of a pulse into two parts, when its normal division would be into three parts, such as in compound meters. p. 95

8 time. Used informally by the authors to refer to any time signature with a lower number (denominator) of 8, i.e. 3/8 time, 5/8 time 6/8 time, etc. p. 52

flag. A hook on a note that shows the note's value. An eighth note has one flag; a sixteenth note, two flags; a thirty-second note, three flags; etc. p. 38

fermata. A sign above or below a note that indicates to hold it longer than its usual duration. It looks like this: ⌢ p. 28

Fine. Literally "The end." It's usually found somewhere other than the last measure of a piece, and indicates the point at which the piece ends. p. 64; p. 90

first, second, third, etc. endings. Alternate endings following a repeated passage. p. 54

4 time. Used informally by the authors to refer to any time signature with a lower number (denominator) of 4; i.e. 4/4 time, 3/4 time 2/4 time, etc. p. 13

Great Divide. A nomenclature unique to the volumes of this book, it refers to divisions between the basic metric groups of two and three notes. p. 26; p. 107

hemiola. A form of syncopation in which the music alternates between pulses of three groups of two and two groups of three. p. 59, p. 93

incomplete measure. A measure with fewer beats than are indicated in the top number (numerator) of the time signature, usually found at the beginning of a piece (See **pickup**). For example, in 3/4 time, a measure with combined notes adding up to less than three quarter notes is incomplete. p. 24

irregular meter. A meter which includes groups of both three and two notes. p. 104

measure. One unit of a meter, delineated by bar lines. Also known as a **bar**. p. 8

meter. The rhythmic ordering of notes into groups of two beats and three beats. p. 8

metric accents. The stronger and weaker accents formed by the groups of two beats and three beats within a measure, which give each meter its own distinct personality. p. 9

offbeat. An un-accented beat in a meter. p. 26

one for nothing, two for nothing, etc. Counting off one, two, etc. measure(s) before starting a piece to establish the meter and tempo. p. 12

out of time. Without any meter, or ignoring the prevailing meter. p. 100

phrase. A small group of notes which form a cohesive pattern together. p. 24

pickup. A partial measure which begins a musical phrase. p. 24

quintuplet. The division of a note or beat into five equal parts. p. 97

repeat signs. Signs that indicate to repeat a section of music. p. 34

rest. A notation indicating a silence for its duration. There is an equivalent rest for each note value. p. 15

Segno. Italian for "Sign." It looks like this: 𝄋 (see **Dal Segno al Fine**). p. 90

septuplet. The division of a note or beat into seven equal parts. p. 97

sextuplet. The division of a note or beat into six equal parts. p. 97

Slap/Clap/Tap. A system of hand-clapping invented by the authors to physically experience the feeling of a meter while reading music. p. 10

syncopation. A rhythm in which the music goes against or between the metric accents, emphasizing **offbeats** or notes between beats. p. 26, p. 68, p. 79

Talking Music. Music compositions with spoken-word texts, written by the authors to practice reading rhythms with Slap/Clap/Tap. p. 12

tempo. The speed at which a piece of music is performed. p 119

tie. A curved line connecting two notes which indicates to hold the tone for the duration of the notes combined, rather than re-articulating the second note. p. 25

time signature. A description of meter, written as a fraction, found at the beginning of a score, and whenever the meter changes. The top number (numerator) gives the number of beats in a measure. The bottom number (denominator) indicates which note has the value of the beat (4 means a quarter note gets the beat; 2 means a half note gets the beat, etc.). p. 8

triplet. The division of a note or beat into three equal parts, usually when its normal division would be 2 or 4. p. 86

tuplet. The division of a note or beat into a particular number of equal parts, different from the normal divisions of a note in that meter, and indicated by that number bracketed above or below the group of notes. When the group of notes is beamed, the number is often shown without a bracket. p. 97

2 time. Used informally by the authors to refer to any time signature with a lower number (denominator) of 2; i.e. 2/2 time, 3/2 time, etc. p. 49

upbeat. A **pickup**. p. 24

verse—refrain. A musical form in which a single refrain (or chorus) is sung (or played) after each of a group of verses. Sometimes the refrain also begins a piece. p. 36

You've Got Rhythm—Order Form

On-Line Orders

To order **You've Got Rhythm** on-line, please visit our web site at: http://www.fleap.com

Telephone and Fax Orders

Call 718-837-0007. Or fax a copy of this completed order form to 718-259-9819.

Mail Orders

Send a copy of this completed order form to Flying Leap Music (see address below)

You've Got Rhythm, Complete (all 3 volumes with 5 extra Talking Music pieces): **$27.95**

You've Got Rhythm, Volumes 1, 2, & 3: $9.95 *per Volume*

Discounts, **Vols. 1, 2 & 3:**	20-34 books: $9.00 each	35-49 books: $7.50 each	50 or more books: $6.00 each

---

_____ copies of **You've Got Rhythm, Complete** ($27.95)	total Complete	
_____ copies of **You've Got Rhythm, Volume 1** ($9.95)	total Vol. 1	
_____ copies of **You've Got Rhythm, Volume 2** ($9.95)	total Vol. 2	
_____ copies of **You've Got Rhythm, Volume 3** ($9.95)	total Vol. 3	
Add 8.25% sales tax (New York only)	Sales Tax	
Shipping and handling: USA: 1-2 books: $5.00, $1.50 each additional. Elsewhere: 1-2 books: $8.00. $2.00 each additional. Call or e-mail for overnight or rush shipping prices .	Shipping	
	Total	

Name:_____

Mailing Address:

_____

_____

City:_____State:_____

Zip:_____Country:_____

Street Address (if different):

_____

_____

City:_____State:_____

Zip:_____Country:_____

E-mail:_____

Telephone:_____

☐ Visa   ☐ Mastercard   ☐ Discover

Credit Card Number:

_____

Expiration Date: _____

or make your check payable to:

flying leap
music
1348 71st Street
Brooklyn, NY 11228
(718) 837-0007
fleap@fleap.com

You may also order at our web site:

http://www.fleap.com